PERSONÆ

—

A DRAFT OF
XXX CANTOS

THE 100 GREATEST MASTERPIECES
OF AMERICAN LITERATURE
a limited edition collection
is published under the auspices of
The American Revolution
Bicentennial Administration

Ezra Pound

PERSONÆ

—

A DRAFT OF XXX CANTOS

Illustrated by Quentin Fiore

A LIMITED EDITION

THE FRANKLIN LIBRARY
FRANKLIN CENTER, PENNSYLVANIA
1981

Contents

PERSONÆ: Collected Shorter Poems of Ezra Pound

Personæ (1908, 1909, 1910)

Ripostes (1912)

Lustra

Cathay

Poems from Blast (1914)

A DRAFT OF XXX CANTOS

PERSONÆ

Collected
Shorter Poems of
Ezra Pound

This book is for
MARY MOORE
of Trenton, if she wants it

PERSONÆ
(1908, 1909, 1910)

THE TREE

I STOOD still and was a tree amid the wood,
Knowing the truth of things unseen before;
Of Daphne and the laurel bow
And that god-feasting couple old
That grew elm-oak amid the wold.
'Twas not until the gods had been
Kindly entreated, and been brought within
Unto the hearth of their heart's home
That they might do this wonder thing;
Nathless I have been a tree amid the wood
And many a new thing understood
That was rank folly to my head before.

THRENOS

NO more for us the little sighing.
No more the winds at twilight trouble us.

Lo the fair dead!

No more do I burn.
No more for us the fluttering of wings
That whirred in the air above us.

Lo the fair dead!

No more desire flayeth me,
No more for us the trembling
At the meeting of hands.

Lo the fair dead!

No more for us the wine of the lips,
No more for us the knowledge.

Lo the fair dead!

No more the torrent,
No more for us the meeting-place
(Lo the fair dead!)
Tintagoel.

LA FRAISNE

FOR I was a gaunt, grave councillor
Being in all things wise, and very old,
But I have put aside this folly and the cold
That old age weareth for a cloak.

I was quite strong—at least they said so—
The young men at the sword-play;
But I have put aside this folly, being gay
In another fashion that more suiteth me.

I have curled 'mid the boles of the ash wood,
I have hidden my face where the oak
Spread his leaves over me, and the yoke
Of the old ways of men have I cast aside.

By the still pool of Mar-nan-otha
Have I found me a bride
That was a dog-wood tree some syne.
She hath called me from mine old ways
She hath hushed my rancour of council,
Bidding me praise

Naught but the wind that flutters in the leaves.

She hath drawn me from mine old ways,
Till men say that I am mad;
But I have seen the sorrow of men, and am glad,
For I know that the wailing and bitterness are a folly.
And I? I have put aside all folly and all grief.
I wrapped my tears in an ellum leaf
And left them under a stone

And now men call me mad because I have thrown
All folly from me, putting it aside
To leave the old barren ways of men,

Because my bride
Is a pool of the wood, and
Though all men say that I am mad
It is only that I am glad,
Very glad, for my bride hath toward me a great love
That is sweeter than the love of women
That plague and burn and drive one away.

Aie-e!   'Tis true that I am gay
    Quite gay, for I have her alone here
    And no man troubleth us.

Once when I was among the young men . . .
And they said I was quite strong, among the young men.
Once there was a woman . . .
. . . but I forget . . . she was . .
. . . I hope she will not come again.

. . . I do not remember . . . . .

I think she hurt me once, but . .
That was very long ago.

I do not like to remember things any more.

I like one little band of winds that blow
In the ash trees here:
For we are quite alone
Here 'mid the ash trees.

CINO

Italian Campagna 1309, *the open road*

BAH!   I have sung women in three cities,
But it is all the same;
And I will sing of the sun.

Lips, words, and you snare them,
Dreams, words, and they are as jewels,
Strange spells of old deity,
Ravens, nights, allurement:
And they are not;
Having become the souls of song.

Eyes, dreams, lips, and the night goes.
Being upon the road once more,
They are not.
Forgetful in their towers of our tuneing
Once for wind-runeing
They dream us-toward and
Sighing, say, "Would Cino,
Passionate Cino, of the wrinkling eyes,
Gay Cino, of quick laugher,
Cino, of the dare, the jibe,
Frail Cino, strongest of his tribe
That tramp old ways beneath the sun-light,
Would Cino of the Luth were here!"

Once, twice, a year—
Vaguely thus word they:

>   "Cino?"   "Oh, eh, Cino Polnesi
>   The singer is't you mean?"
>   "Ah yes, passed once our way,
>   A saucy fellow, but . . .
>   (Oh they are all one these vagabonds),
>   Peste! 'tis his own songs?
>   Or some other's that he sings?
>   But *you*, My Lord, how with your city?"

But you "My Lord," God's pity!
And all I knew were out, My Lord, you
Were Lack-land Cino, e'en as I am,
O Sinistro.

I have sung women in three cities.
But it is all one.
I will sing of the sun.
    . . . eh? . . . they mostly had grey eyes,
But it is all one, I will sing of the sun.

> "'Pollo Phoibee, old tin pan, you
> Glory to Zeus' aegis-day,
> Shield o' steel-blue, th' heaven o'er us
> Hath for boss thy lustre gay!
>
> 'Pollo Phoibee, to our way-fare
> Make thy laugh our wander-lied;
> Bid thy 'fulgence bear away care.
> Cloud and rain-tears pass they fleet!
>
> Seeking e'er the new-laid rast-way
> To the gardens of the sun . . .
>   .   .   .   .   .   .
> I have sung women in three cities
> But it is all one.
>
> I will sing of the white birds
> In the blue waters of heaven,
> The clouds that are spray to its sea."

NA AUDIART

Que be-m vols mal

NOTE: Anyone who has read anything of the troubadours knows well the tale of Bertran of Born and My Lady Maent of Montagnac, and knows also the song he made when she would none of him, the song wherein he, seeking to find or make her equal, begs of each preëminent lady of Langue d'Oc some trait or some fair semblance: thus of Cembelins her "esgart amoros" to wit, her love-lit glance, of Aelis her speech free-running, of the Vicomtess of Chalais her throat and her two hands, at Roacoart of Anhes her hair golden as Iseult's; and even in this fashion of Lady Audiart "although she would that ill come unto him" he sought and praised the lineaments of the torse. And all this to make "Una dompna soiseubuda" a borrowed lady or as the Italians translated it "Una donna ideale."

THOUGH thou well dost wish me ill
            Audiart, Audiart,
Where thy bodice laces start
As ivy fingers clutching through
Its crevices,
            Audiart, Audiart,
Stately, tall and lovely tender
Who shall render
            Audiart, Audiart,
Praises meet unto thy fashion?
Here a word kiss!
            Pass I on
Unto Lady "Miels-de-Ben,"
Having praised thy girdle's scope
How the stays ply back from it;
I breathe no hope
That thou shouldst . . .
            Nay no whit
Bespeak thyself for anything.
Just a word in thy praise, girl,
Just for the swirl
Thy satins make upon the stair,
'Cause never a flaw was there
Where thy torse and limbs are met
Though thou hate me, read it set
In rose and gold.*

* I.e., in illumed manuscript.

Or when the minstrel, tale half told,
Shall burst to lilting at the praise
                    "Audiart, Audiart" . . .
Bertrans, master of his lays,
Bertrans of Aultaforte thy praise
Sets forth, and though thou hate me well,
Yea though thou wish me ill,
                    Audiart, Audiart.
Thy loveliness is here writ till,
                    Audiart,
Oh, till thou come again.**
And being bent and wrinkled, in a form
That hath no perfect limning, when the warm
Youth dew is cold
Upon thy hands, and thy old soul
Scorning a new, wry'd casement,
Churlish at seemed misplacement,
Finds the earth as bitter
As now seems it sweet,
Being so young and fair
As then only in dreams,
Being then young and wry'd,
Broken of ancient pride,
Thou shalt then soften,
Knowing, I know not how,
Thou wert once she
                    Audiart, Audiart
For whose fairness one forgave
                    Audiart,
Audiart
        Que be-m vols mal.

** Reincarnate.

VILLONAUD FOR THIS YULE

TOWARDS the Noel that morte saison
(*Christ make the shepherds' homage dear!*)
Then when the grey wolves everychone
Drink of the winds their chill small-beer
And lap o' the snows food's gueredon
Then makyth my heart his yule-tide cheer
(Skoal! with the dregs if the clear be gone!)
Wining the ghosts of yester-year.

Ask ye what ghosts I dream upon?
(*What of the magians' scented gear?*)
The ghosts of dead loves everyone
That make the stark winds reek with fear
Lest love return with the foison sun
And slay the memories that me cheer
(Such as I drink to mine fashion)
Wining the ghosts of yester-year.

Where are the joys my heart had won?
(*Saturn and Mars to Zeus drawn near!*)*
Where are the lips mine lay upon,
Aye! where are the glances feat and clear
That bade my heart his valour don?
I skoal to the eyes as grey-blown mere
(Who knows whose was that paragon?)
Wining the ghosts of yester-year.

Prince: ask me not what I have done
Nor what God hath that can me cheer
But ye ask first where the winds are gone
Wining the ghosts of yester-year.

* *Signum Nativitatis.*

A VILLONAUD: BALLAD OF THE GIBBET

OR THE SONG OF THE SIXTH COMPANION

SCENE: *"En ce bourdel où tenons nostre estat."*
It being remembered that there were six of us with Master Villon, when that expecting presently to be hanged he writ a ballad whereof ye know:
"Frères humains qui après nous vivez."

DRINK ye a skoal for the gallows tree!
François and Margot and thee and me,
Drink we the comrades merrily
That said us, "Till then" for the gallows tree!

Fat Pierre with the hook gauche-main,
Thomas Larron "Ear-the-less,"
Tybalde and that armouress
Who gave this poignard its premier stain
Pinning the Guise that had been fain
To make him a mate of the "Haulte Noblesse"
And bade her be out with ill address
As a fool that mocketh his drue's disdeign.

Drink we a skoal for the gallows tree!
François and Margot and thee and me,
Drink we to Marienne Ydole,
That hell brenn not her o'er cruelly.

Drink we the lusty robbers twain,
Black is the pitch o' their wedding dress,*
Lips shrunk back for the wind's caress
As lips shrink back when we feel the strain
Of love that loveth in hell's disdeign,
And sense the teeth through the lips that press
'Gainst our lips for the soul's distress
That striveth to ours across the pain.

---

* Certain gibbeted corpses used to be coated with tar as a preservative; thus one scarecrow served as warning for considerable time. See Hugo, *L'Homme qui Rit.*

Drink we skoal to the gallows tree!
François and Margot and thee and me,
For Jehan and Raoul de Vallerie
Whose frames have the night and its winds in fee.

Maturin, Guillaume, Jacques d'Allmain,
Culdou lacking a coat to bless
One lean moiety of his nakedness
That plundered St. Hubert back o' the fane:
Aie! the lean bare tree is widowed again
For Michault le Borgne that would confess
In "faith and troth" to a traitoress,
"Which of his brothers had he slain?"

But drink we skoal to the gallows tree!
François and Margot and thee and me:

These that we loved shall God love less
And smite always at their faibleness?

Skoal!! to the gallows! and then pray we:
God damn his hell out speedily
And bring their souls to his "Haulte Citee."

MESMERISM

"And a cat's in the water-butt." —ROBERT BROWNING

AYE you're a man that! ye old mesmerizer
Tyin' your meanin' in seventy swadelin's,
One must of needs be a hang'd early riser
To catch you at worm turning.   Holy Odd's bodykins!

"Cat's i' the water butt!"   Thought's in your verse-barrel,
Tell us this thing rather, then we'll believe you,
You, Master Bob Browning, spite your apparel
Jump to your sense and give praise as we'd lief do.

You wheeze as a head-cold long-tonsilled Calliope,
But God! what a sight you ha' got o' our in'ards,

Mad as a hatter but surely no Myope,
Broad as all ocean and leanin' man-kin'ards.

Heart that was big as the bowels of Vesuvius,
Words that were wing'd as her sparks in eruption,
Eagled and thundered as Jupiter Pluvius,
Sound in your wind past all signs o' corruption.

Here's to you, Old Hippety-Hop o' the accents,
True to the Truth's sake and crafty dissector,
You grabbed at the gold sure; had no need to pack cents
Into your versicles.
                    Clear sight's elector!

FAMAM LIBROSQUE CANO

YOUR songs?
                    Oh!   The little mothers
Will sing them in the twilight,
And when the night
Shrinketh the kiss of the dawn
That loves and kills,
What times the swallow fills
Her note, the little rabbit folk
That some call children,
Such as are up and wide,
Will laugh your verses to each other,
Pulling on their shoes for the day's business,
Serious child business that the world
Laughs at, and grows stale;
Such is the tale
—Part of it—of thy song-life.

Mine?

        A book is known by them that read
        That same.   Thy public in my screed
        Is listed.   Well!   Some score years hence

Behold mine audience,
As we had seen him yesterday.

Scrawny, be-spectacled, out at heels,
Such an one as the world feels
A sort of curse against its guzzling
And its age-lasting wallow for red greed
And yet; full speed
Though it should run for its own getting,
Will turn aside to sneer at
'Cause he hath
No coin, no will to snatch the aftermath
Of Mammon
Such an one as women draw away from
For the tobacco ashes scattered on his coat
And sith his throat
Shows razor's unfamiliarity
And three days' beard;

Such an one picking a ragged
Backless copy from the stall,
Too cheap for cataloguing,
Loquitur,

"Ah-eh! the strange rare name . . .
Ah-eh! He must be rare if even *I* have not . . ."
And lost mid-page
Such age
As his pardons the habit,
He analyses form and thought to see
How I 'scaped immortality.

PRAISE OF YSOLT

IN vain have I striven
        to teach my heart to bow;
In vain have I said to him
"There be many singers greater than thou."

But his answer cometh, as winds and as lutany,
As a vague crying upon the night
That leaveth me no rest, saying ever,
        "Song, a song."

Their echoes play upon each other in the twilight
Seeking ever a song.
Lo, I am worn with travail
And the wandering of many roads hath made my eyes
As dark red circles filled with dust.
Yet there is a trembling upon me in the twilight,
    And little red elf words crying "A song,"
    Little grey elf words crying for a song,
    Little brown leaf words crying "A song,"
    Little green leaf words crying for a song.
The words are as leaves, old brown leaves in the spring time
Blowing they know not whither, seeking a song.

White words as snow flakes but they are cold,
Moss words, lip words, words of slow streams.

In vain have I striven
        to teach my soul to bow,
In vain have I pled with him:
    "There be greater souls than thou."

For in the morn of my years there came a woman
As moonlight calling,
As the moon calleth the tides,
        "Song, a song."

Wherefore I made her a song and she went from me
As the moon doth from the sea,
But still came the leaf words, little brown elf words
Saying "The soul sendeth us."
                              "A song, a song!"
And in vain I cried unto them "I have no song
For she I sang of hath gone from me."

But my soul sent a woman, a woman of the wonder-folk
A woman as fire upon the pine woods
            crying "Song, a song."
As the flame crieth unto the sap.
My song was ablaze with her and she went from me
As flame leaveth the embers so went she unto new forests
And the words were with me
            crying ever "Song, a song."

And I "I have no song,"
Till my soul sent a woman as the sun:
Yea as the sun calleth to the seed,
As the spring upon the bough
So is she that cometh, the mother of songs,
She that holdeth the wonder words within her eyes
The words, little elf words
            that call ever unto me,
                              "Song, a song."

In vain have I striven with my soul
            to teach my soul to bow.
What soul boweth
            while in his heart art thou?

DE AEGYPTO

I EVEN I, am he who knoweth the roads
Through the sky, and the wind thereof is my body.

I have beheld the Lady of Life,
I, even I, who fly with the swallows.

Green and gray is her raiment,
Trailing along the wind.

I, even I, am he who knoweth the roads
Through the sky, and the wind thereof is my body.

Manus animam pinxit,
My pen is in my hand

To write the acceptable word. . . .
My mouth to chant the pure singing!

Who hath the mouth to receive it,
The song of the Lotus of Kumi?

I, even I, am he who knoweth the roads
Through the sky, and the wind thereof is my body.

I am flame that riseth in the sun,
I, even I, who fly with the swallows.

The moon is upon my forehead,
The winds are under my lips.

The moon is a great pearl in the waters of sapphire,
Cool to my fingers the flowing waters.

I, even I, am he who knoweth the roads
Through the sky, and the wind thereof is my body.

FOR E. McC.

That was my counter-blade under Leonardo Terrone,
Master of Fence

GONE while your tastes were keen to you,
Gone where the grey winds call to you,
  By that high fencer, even Death,
Struck of the blade that no man parrieth;
Such is your fence, one saith,
  One that hath known you.
Drew you your sword most gallantly
Made you your pass most valiantly
  'Gainst that grey fencer, even Death.

Gone as a gust of breath
Faith! no man tarrieth,
"Se il cor ti manca," but it failed thee not!
"Non ti fidar," it is the sword that speaks
"In me."*

Thou trusted'st in thyself and met the blade
'Thout mask or gauntlet, and art laid
As memorable broken blades that be
Kept as bold trophies of old pageantry.
As old Toledos past their days of war
Are kept mnemonic of the strokes they bore,
So art thou with us, being good to keep
In our heart's sword-rack, though thy sword-arm sleep.

Envoi

Struck of the blade that no man parrieth
Pierced of the point that toucheth lastly all,
'Gainst that grey fencer, even Death,
Behold the shield!   He shall not take thee all.

---

* Sword-rune "If thy heart fail thee trust not in me."

: 20 :

IN DURANCE

(1907)

I AM homesick after mine own kind,
Oh I know that there are folk about me, friendly faces,
But I am homesick after mine own kind.

"These sell our pictures"! Oh well,
They reach me not, touch me some edge or that,
But reach me not and all my life's become
One flame, that reaches not beyond
My heart's own hearth,
Or hides among the ashes there for thee.
"Thee"? Oh, "Thee" is who cometh first
Out of mine own soul-kin,
For I am homesick after mine own kind
And ordinary people touch me not.
                                          And I am homesick

After mine own kind that know, and feel
And have some breath for beauty and the arts.

Aye, I am wistful for my kin of the spirit
And have none about me save in the shadows
When come *they*, surging of power, "DAEMON,"
"Quasi KALOUN."   S.T. says Beauty is most that, a "calling to the
        soul."
Well then, so call they, the swirlers out of the mist of my soul,
They that come mewards, bearing old magic.

But for all that, I am homesick after mine own kind
And would meet kindred even as I am,
Flesh-shrouded bearing the secret.
"All they that with strange sadness"
Have the earth in mockery, and are kind to all,
My fellows, aye I know the glory

Of th' unbounded ones, but ye, that hide
As I hide most the while
And burst forth to the windows only whiles or whiles

For love, or hope, or beauty or for power,
Then smoulder, with the lids half closed
And are untouched by echoes of the world.

Oh ye, my fellows: with the seas between us some be,
Purple and sapphire for the silver shafts
Of sun and spray all shattered at the bows;
And some the hills hold off,
The little hills to east of us, though here we
Have damp and plain to be our shutting in.

And yet my soul sings "Up!" and we are one.
Yea thou, and Thou, and THOU, and all my kin
To whom my breast and arms are ever warm,
For that I love ye as the wind the trees
That holds their blossoms and their leaves in cure
And calls the utmost singing from the boughs
That 'thout him, save the aspen, were as dumb
Still shade, and bade no whisper speak the birds of how
"Beyond, beyond, beyond, there lies . . ."

MARVOIL

A POOR clerk I, "Arnaut the less" they call me,
And because I have small mind to sit
Day long, long day cooped on a stool
A-jumbling o' figures for Maître Jacques Polin,
I ha' taken to rambling the South here.

The Vicomte of Beziers 's not such a bad lot.
I made rimes to his lady this three year:
Vers and canzone, till that damn'd son of Aragon,
Alfonso the half-bald, took to hanging
His helmet at Beziers.
Then came what might come, to wit: three men and one woman,
Beziers off at Mont-Ausier, I and his lady
Singing the stars in the turrets of Beziers,

And one lean Aragonese cursing the seneschal
To the end that you see, friends:

Aragon cursing in Aragon, Beziers busy at Beziers—
Bored to an inch of extinction,
Tibors all tongue and temper at Mont-Ausier,
Me! in this damn'd inn of Avignon,
Stringing long verse for the Burlatz;
All for one half-bald, knock-knee'd king of the Aragonese,
Alfonso, Quattro, poke-nose.

And if when I am dead
They take the trouble to tear out this wall here,
They'll know more of Arnaut of Marvoil
Than half his canzoni say of him.
As for will and testament I leave none,
Save this: "Vers and canzone to the Countess of Beziers

In return for the first kiss she gave me."
May her eyes and her cheek be fair
To all men except the King of Aragon,
And may I come speedily to Beziers
Whither my desire and my dream have preceded me.

O hole in the wall here! be thou my jongleur
As ne'er had I other, and when the wind blows,
Sing thou the grace of the Lady of Beziers,
For even as thou art hollow before I fill thee with this parchment,
So is my heart hollow when she filleth not mine eyes,
And so were my mind hollow, did she not fill utterly my thought.

Wherefore, O hole in the wall here,
When the wind blows sigh thou for my sorrow
That I have not the Countess of Beziers
Close in my arms here.
Even as thou shalt soon have this parchment.

O hole in the wall here, be thou my jongleur,
And though thou sighest my sorrow in the wind,
Keep yet my secret in thy breast here;
Even as I keep her image in my heart here.

Mihi pergamena deest

AND THUS IN NINEVEH

"AYE!   I am a poet and upon my tomb
Shall maidens scatter rose leaves
And men myrtles, ere the night
Slays day with her dark sword.

"Lo! this thing is not mine
Nor thine to hinder,
For the custom is full old,
And here in Nineveh have I beheld
Many a singer pass and take his place
In those dim halls where no man troubleth
His sleep or song.
And many a one hath sung his songs
More craftily, more subtle-souled than I;
And many a one now doth surpass
My wave-worn beauty with his wind of flowers,
Yet am I poet, and upon my tomb
Shall all men scatter rose leaves
Ere the night slay light
With her blue sword.

"It is not, Raana, that my song rings highest
Or more sweet in tone than any, but that I
Am here a Poet, that doth drink of life
As lesser men drink wine."

THE WHITE STAG

I HA' seen them 'mid the clouds on the heather.
Lo! they pause not for love nor for sorrow,
Yet their eyes are as the eyes of a maid to her lover,
When the white hart breaks his cover
And the white wind breaks the morn.

> *"'Tis the white stag, Fame, we're a-hunting,*
> *Bid the world's hounds come to horn!"*

GUIDO INVITES YOU THUS*

"LAPPO I leave behind and Dante too,
Lo, I would sail the seas with thee alone!
Talk me no love talk, no bought-cheap fiddl'ry,
Mine is the ship and thine the merchandise,
All the blind earth knows not th'emprise
Whereto thou calledst and whereto I call.

Lo, I have seen thee bound about with dreams,
Lo, I have known thy heart and its desire;
Life, all of it, my sea, and all men's streams
Are fused in it as flames of an altar fire!
Lo, thou hast voyaged not!   The ship is mine."

* The reference is to Dante's sonnet "Guido vorrei . . ."

NIGHT LITANY

O DIEU, purifiez nos cœurs!
        Purifiez nos cœurs!

Yea the lines hast thou laid unto me
        in pleasant places,
And the beauty of this thy Venice
        hast thou shown unto me
Until is its loveliness become unto me
        a thing of tears.

O God, what great kindness
        have we done in times past
        and forgotten it,
That thou givest this wonder unto us,
        O God of waters?

O God of the night,
        What great sorrow
Cometh unto us,
        That thou thus repayest us
Before the time of its coming?

O God of silence,
        Purifiez nos cœurs,
        Purifiez nos cœurs,
For we have seen
The glory of the shadow of the
        likeness of thine handmaid,

Yea, the glory of the shadow
        of thy Beauty hath walked
Upon the shadow of the waters
In this thy Venice.
        And before the holiness
Of the shadow of thy handmaid
    Have I hidden mine eyes,
        O God of waters.

O God of silence,
        Purifiez nos cœurs,
        Purifiez nos cœurs,
O God of waters,
        make clean our hearts within us,
        For I have seen the
Shadow of this thy Venice
Floating upon the waters,
        And thy stars

Have seen this thing, out of their far courses
Have they seen this thing,
        O God of waters,
Even as are thy stars
Silent unto us in their far-coursing,
Even so is mine heart
        become silent within me.

        Purifiez nos cœurs
O God of the silence,
        Purifiez nos cœurs
O God of waters.

SESTINA: ALTAFORTE

LOQUITUR: *En* Bertrans de Born.
Dante Alighieri put this man in hell for that he was
a stirrer up of strife.
Eccovi!
Judge ye!
Have I dug him up again?
The scene is at his castle, Altaforte.   "Papiols" is his jongleur.
"The Leopard," the *device* of Richard Cœur de Lion.

I

DAMN it all! all this our South stinks peace.
You whoreson dog, Papiols, come!   Let's to music!
I have no life save when the swords clash.
But ah! when I see the standards gold, vair, purple, opposing
And the broad fields beneath them turn crimson,
Then howl I my heart nigh mad with rejoicing.

II

In hot summer have I great rejoicing
When the tempests kill the earth's foul peace,
And the lightnings from black heav'n flash crimson,
And the fierce thunders roar me their music
And the winds shriek through the clouds mad, opposing,
And through all the riven skies God's swords clash.

III

Hell grant soon we hear again the swords clash!
And the shrill neighs of destriers in battle rejoicing,
Spiked breast to spiked breast opposing!
Better one hour's stour than a year's peace
With fat boards, bawds, wine and frail music!
Bah! there's no wine like the blood's crimson!

IV

And I love to see the sun rise blood-crimson.
And I watch his spears through the dark clash
And it fills all my heart with rejoicing
And pries wide my mouth with fast music

When I see him so scorn and defy peace,
His lone might 'gainst all darkness opposing.

V

The man who fears war and squats opposing
My words for stour, hath no blood of crimson
But is fit only to rot in womanish peace
Far from where worth's won and the swords clash
For the death of such sluts I go rejoicing;
Yea, I fill all the air with my music.

VI

Papiols, Papiols, to the music!
There's no sound like to swords swords opposing,
No cry like the battle's rejoicing
When our elbows and swords drip the crimson
And our charges 'gainst "The Leopard's" rush clash.
May God damn for ever all who cry "Peace!"

VII

And let the music of the swords make them crimson!
Hell grant soon we hear again the swords clash!
Hell blot black for alway the thought "Peace"!

PIERE VIDAL OLD

It is of Piere Vidal, the fool *par excellence* of all Provence, of whom the tale tells how
he ran mad, as a wolf, because of his love for Loba of Penautier, and how men
hunted him with dogs through the mountains of Cabaret and brought him for dead
to the dwelling of this Loba (she-wolf) of Penautier, and how she and her Lord had
him healed and made welcome, and he stayed some time at that court. He speaks:

WHEN I but think upon the great dead days
And turn my mind upon that splendid madness,
Lo! I do curse my strength
And blame the sun his gladness;
For that the one is dead
And the red sun mocks my sadness.

Behold me, Vidal, that was fool of fools!
Swift as the king wolf was I and as strong
When tall stags fled me through the alder brakes,
And every jongleur knew me in his song,
And the hounds fled and the deer fled
And none fled over-long.

Even the grey pack knew me and knew fear.
God! how the swiftest hind's blood spurted hot
Over the sharpened teeth and purpling lips!
Hot was that hind's blood yet it scorched me not
As did first scorn, then lips of the Penautier!
Aye ye are fools, if ye think time can blot

From Piere Vidal's remembrance that blue night.
God! but the purple of the sky was deep!
Clear, deep, translucent, so the stars me seemed
Set deep in crystal; and because my sleep
—Rare visitor—came not,—the Saints I guerdon
For that restlessness—Piere set to keep

One more fool's vigil with the hollyhocks.
Swift came the Loba, as a branch that's caught,
Torn, green and silent in the swollen Rhone,
Green was her mantle, close, and wrought

Of some thin silk stuff that's scarce stuff at all,
But like a mist wherethrough her white form fought,

And conquered!   Ah God! conquered!
Silent my mate came as the night was still.
Speech? Words? Faugh! Who talks of words and love?!
Hot is such love and silent,
Silent as fate is, and as strong until
It faints in taking and in giving all.

Stark, keen, triumphant, till it plays at death.
God! she was white then, splendid as some tomb
High wrought of marble, and the panting breath
Ceased utterly.   Well, then I waited, drew,
Half-sheathed, then naked from its saffron sheath
Drew full this dagger that doth tremble here.

Just then she woke and mocked the less keen blade.
Ah God, the Loba! and my only mate!
Was there such flesh made ever and unmade!
God curse the years that turn such women grey!
Behold here Vidal, that was hunted, flayed,
Shamed and yet bowed not and that won at last.

And yet I curse the sun for his red gladness,
I that have known strath, garth, brake, dale,
And every run-away of the wood through that great madness,
Behold me shrivelled as an old oak's trunk
And made men's mock'ry in my rotten sadness!

No man hath heard the glory of my days:
No man hath dared and won his dare as I:
One night, one body and one welding flame!
What do ye own, ye niggards! that can buy
Such glory of the earth?   Or who will win
Such battle-guerdon with his "prowesse high"?

O Age gone lax!   O stunted followers,
That mask at passions and desire desires,

Behold me shrivelled, and your mock of mocks;
And yet I mock you by the mighty fires
That burnt me to this ash.
.   .   .   .
Ah!   Cabaret!   Ah Cabaret, thy hills again!
.   .   .   .
Take your hands off me! . . .   [*Sniffing the air.*
                              Ha! this scent is hot!

PARACELSUS IN EXCELSIS

"BEING no longer human, why should I
Pretend humanity or don the frail attire?
Men have I known and men, but never one
Was grown so free an essence, or become
So simply element as what I am.
The mist goes from the mirror and I see.
Behold! the world of forms is swept beneath—
Turmoil grown visible beneath our peace,
And we that are grown formless, rise above—
Fluids intangible that have been men,
We seem as statues round whose high-risen base
Some overflowing river is run mad,
In us alone the element of calm."

BALLAD OF THE GOODLY FERE

Simon Zelotes speaketh it somewhile after the Crucifixion
Fere = Mate, Companion.

HA' we lost the goodliest fere o' all
For the priests and the gallows tree?
Aye lover he was of brawny men,
O' ships and the open sea.

When they came wi' a host to take Our Man
His smile was good to see,
"First let these go!" quo' our Goodly Fere,
"Or I'll see ye damned," says he.

Aye he sent us out through the crossed high spears
And the scorn of his laugh rang free,
"Why took ye not me when I walked about
Alone in the town?" says he.

Oh we drunk his "Hale" in the good red wine
When we last made company,
No capon priest was the Goodly Fere
But a man o' men was he.

I ha' seen him drive a hundred men
Wi' a bundle o' cords swung free,
That they took the high and holy house
For their pawn and treasury.

They'll no' get him a' in a book I think
Though they write it cunningly;
No mouse of the scrolls was the Goodly Fere
But aye loved the open sea.

If they think they ha' snared our Goodly Fere
They are fools to the last degree.
"I'll go to the feast," quo' our Goodly Fere,
"Though I go to the gallows tree."

"Ye ha' seen me heal the lame and blind,
And wake the dead," says he,
"Ye shall see one thing to master all:
'Tis how a brave man dies on the tree."

A son of God was the Goodly Fere
That bade us his brothers be.
I ha' seen him cow a thousand men.
I have seen him upon the tree.

He cried no cry when they drave the nails
And the blood gushed hot and free,
The hounds of the crimson sky gave tongue
But never a cry cried he.

I ha' seen him cow a thousand men
On the hills o' Galilee,
They whined as he walked out calm between,
Wi' his eyes like the grey o' the sea,

Like the sea that brooks no voyaging
With the winds unleashed and free,
Like the sea that he cowed at Genseret
Wi' twey words spoke' suddently.

A master of men was the Goodly Fere,
A mate of the wind and sea,
If they think they ha' slain our Goodly Fere
They are fools eternally.

I ha' seen him eat o' the honey-comb
Sin' they nailed him to the tree.

ON HIS OWN FACE IN A GLASS

O STRANGE face there in the glass!
O ribald company, O saintly host,
O sorrow-swept my fool,
What answer? O ye myriad
That strive and play and pass,
Jest, challenge, counterlie!
I? I? I?
      And ye?

THE EYES

REST Master, for we be a-weary, weary
And would feel the fingers of the wind
Upon these lids that lie over us
Sodden and lead-heavy.

     Rest brother, for lo! the dawn is without!
The yellow flame paleth
And the wax runs low.

Free us, for without be goodly colours,
Green of the wood-moss and flower colours,
And coolness beneath the trees.

     Free us, for we perish
In this ever-flowing monotony
Of ugly print marks, black
Upon white parchment.

     Free us, for there is one
Whose smile more availeth
Than all the age-old knowledge of thy books:
And we would look thereon.

FRANCESCA

YOU came in out of the night
And there were flowers in your hands,
Now you will come out of a confusion of people,
Out of a turmoil of speech about you.

I who have seen you amid the primal things
Was angry when they spoke your name
In ordinary places.
I would that the cool waves might flow over my mind,
And that the world should dry as a dead leaf,
Or as a dandelion seed-pod and be swept away,
So that I might find you again,
Alone.

PLANH FOR THE YOUNG ENGLISH KING

That is, Prince Henry Plantagenet, elder brother to Richard Cœur de Lion.
From the Provençal of Bertrans de Born
"Si tuit li dolh elh plor elh marrimen."

IF all the grief and woe and bitterness,
All dolour, ill and every evil chance
That ever came upon this grieving world
Were set together they would seem but light
Against the death of the young English King.
Worth lieth riven and Youth dolorous,
The world o'ershadowed, soiled and overcast,
Void of all joy and full of ire and sadness.

Grieving and sad and full of bitterness
Are left in teen the liegemen courteous,
The joglars supple and the troubadours.
O'er much hath ta'en Sir Death that deadly warrior
In taking from them the young English King,
Who made the freest hand seem covetous.
'Las! Never was nor will be in this world
The balance for this loss in ire and sadness!

O skillful Death and full of bitterness,
Well mayst thou boast that thou the best chevalier
That any folk e'er had, hast from us taken;
Sith nothing is that unto worth pertaineth
But had its life in the young English King
And better were it, should God grant his pleasure,
That he should live than many a living dastard
That doth but wound the good with ire and sadness.

From this faint world, how full of bitterness
Love takes his way and holds his joy deceitful,
Sith no thing is but turneth unto anguish
And each to-day 'vails less than yestere'en,
Let each man visage this young English King
That was most valiant 'mid all worthiest men!
Gone is his body fine and amorous,
Whence have we grief, discord and deepest sadness.

Him, whom it pleased for our great bitterness
To come to earth to draw us from misventure,
Who drank of death for our salvacioun,
Him do we pray as to a Lord most righteous
And humble eke, that the young English King
He please to pardon, as true pardon is,
And bid go in with honourèd companions
There where there is no grief, nor shall be sadness.

BALLATETTA

THE light became her grace and dwelt among
Blind eyes and shadows that are formed as men;
Lo, how the light doth melt us into song:

The broken sunlight for a helm she beareth
Who hath my heart in jurisdiction.
In wild-wood never fawn nor fallow fareth
So silent light; no gossamer is spun
So delicate as she is, when the sun
Drives the clear emeralds from the bended grasses
Lest they should parch too swiftly, where she passes.

PRAYER FOR HIS LADY'S LIFE

From Propertius, Elegiae, lib. III, 26

HERE let thy clemency, Persephone, hold firm,
Do thou, Pluto, bring here no greater harshness.
So many thousand beauties are gone down to Avernus,
Ye might let one remain above with us.

With you is Iope, with you the white-gleaming Tyro,
With you is Europa and the shameless Pasiphae,
And all the fair from Troy and all from Achaia,
From the sundered realms, of Thebes and of aged Priamus;
And all the maidens of Rome, as many as they were,
They died and the greed of your flame consumes them.

Here let thy clemency, Persephone, hold firm,
Do thou, Pluto, bring here no greater harshness.
So many thousand fair are gone down to Avernus,
Ye might let one remain above with us.

SPEECH FOR PSYCHE
IN THE GOLDEN BOOK OF APULEIUS

ALL night, and as the wind lieth among
The cypress trees, he lay,
Nor held me save as air that brusheth by one
Close, and as the petals of flowers in falling
Waver and seem not drawn to earth, so he
Seemed over me to hover light as leaves
And closer me than air,
And music flowing through me seemed to open
Mine eyes upon new colours.
O winds, what wind can match the weight of him!

"BLANDULA, TENELLA, VAGULA"

WHAT hast thou, O my soul, with paradise?
Will we not rather, when our freedom's won,
Get us to some clear place wherein the sun
Lets drift in on us through the olive leaves
A liquid glory?   If at Sirmio,
My soul, I meet thee, when this life's outrun,
Will we not find some headland consecrated
By aery apostles of terrene delight,
Will not our cult be founded on the waves,
Clear sapphire, cobalt, cyanine,
On triune azures, the impalpable
Mirrors unstill of the eternal change?

Soul, if She meet us there, will any rumour
Of havens more high and courts desirable
Lure us beyond the cloudy peak of Riva?

ERAT HORA

"THANK you, whatever comes." And then she turned
And, as the ray of sun on hanging flowers
Fades when the wind hath lifted them aside,
Went swiftly from me. Nay, whatever comes
One hour was sunlit and the most high gods
May not make boast of any better thing
Than to have watched that hour as it passed.

ROME

FROM THE FRENCH OF JOACHIM DU BELLAY

"Troica Roma resurges."
PROPERTIUS

O THOU new comer who seek'st Rome in Rome
And find'st in Rome no thing thou canst call Roman;
Arches worn old and palaces made common,
Rome's name alone within these walls keeps home.

Behold how pride and ruin can befall
One who hath set the whole world 'neath her laws,
All-conquering, now conquerèd, because
She is Time's prey and Time consumeth all.

Rome that art Rome's one sole last monument,
Rome that alone hast conquered Rome the town,
Tiber alone, transient and seaward bent,
Remains of Rome. O world, thou unconstant mime!
That which stands firm in thee Time batters down,
And that which fleeteth doth outrun swift time.

HER MONUMENT,
THE IMAGE CUT THEREON

FROM THE ITALIAN OF LEOPARDI

SUCH wast thou,
Who art now
But buried dust and rusted skeleton.
Above the bones and mire,
Motionless, placed in vain,
Mute mirror of the flight of speeding years,
Sole guard of grief
Sole guard of memory
Standeth this image of the beauty sped.

O glance, when thou wast still as thou art now,
How hast thou set the fire
A-tremble in men's veins; O lip curved high
To mind me of some urn of full delight,
O throat girt round of old with swift desire,
O palms of Love, that in your wonted ways
Not once but many a day
Felt hands turn ice a-sudden, touching ye,
That ye were once! of all the grace ye had
That which remaineth now
Shameful, most sad
Finds 'neath this rock fit mould, fit resting place!

And still when fate recalleth,
Even that semblance that appears amongst us
Is like to heaven's most 'live imagining.
All, all our life's eternal mystery!
To-day, on high
Mounts, from our mighty thoughts and from the fount
Of sense untellable, Beauty
That seems to be some quivering splendour cast
By the immortal nature on this quicksand,

And by surhuman fates
Given to mortal state
To be a sign and an hope made secure
Of blissful kingdoms and the aureate spheres;
And on the morrow, by some lightsome twist,
Shameful in sight, abject, abominable
All this angelic aspect can return
And be but what it was
With all the admirable concepts that moved from it
Swept from the mind with it in its departure.

Infinite things desired, lofty visions
'Got on desirous thought by natural virtue,
And the wise concord, whence through delicious seas
The arcane spirit of the whole Mankind
Turns hardy pilot . . . and if one wrong note
Strike the tympanum,
Instantly
That paradise is hurled to nothingness.

O mortal nature,
If thou art
Frail and so vile in all,
How canst thou reach so high with thy poor sense;
Yet if thou art
Noble in any part
How is the noblest of thy speech and thought
So lightly wrought
Or to such base occasion lit and quenched?

SATIEMUS

WHAT if I know thy speeches word by word?
And if thou knew'st I knew them wouldst thou speak?
What if I know thy speeches word by word,
And all the time thou sayest them o'er I said,
"Lo, one there was who bent her fair bright head,
Sighing as thou dost through the golden speech."
Or, as our laughters mingle each with each,
As crushed lips take their respite fitfully,
What if my thoughts were turned in their mid reach
Whispering among them, "The fair dead
Must know such moments, thinking on the grass;
On how white dogwoods murmured overhead
In the bright glad days!"
How if the low dear sound within thy throat
Hath as faint lute-strings in its dim accord
Dim tales that blind me, running one by one
With times told over as we tell by rote;
What if I know thy laughter word by word
Nor find aught novel in thy merriment?

MR. HOUSMAN'S MESSAGE

O WOE, woe,
People are born and die,
We also shall be dead pretty soon
Therefore let us act as if we were
                 dead already.

The bird sits on the hawthorn tree
But he dies also, presently.
Some lads get hung, and some get shot,
Woeful is this human lot.
              Woe! woe, etcetera. . . .

London is a woeful place,
Shropshire is much pleasanter.
Then let us smile a little space
Upon fond nature's morbid grace.
          Oh, Woe, woe, woe, etcetera. . . .

TRANSLATIONS AND ADAPTATIONS FROM HEINE

FROM "DIE HEIMKEHR"

I

IS your hate, then, of such measure?
Do you, truly, so detest me?
Through all the world will I complain
Of *how* you have addressed me.

O ye lips that are ungrateful,
Hath it never once distressed you,
That you can say such *awful* things
Of *any* one who ever kissed you?

II

SO thou hast forgotten fully
That I so long held thy heart wholly,
Thy little heart, so sweet and false and small
That there's no thing more sweet or false at all.

Love and lay thou hast forgotten fully,
And my heart worked at them unduly.
I know not if the love or if the lay were better stuff,
But I know now, they both were good enough.

III

TELL me where thy lovely love is,
Whom thou once did sing so sweetly,
When the fairy flames enshrouded
Thee, and held thy heart completely.

All the flames are dead and sped now
And my heart is cold and sere;
Behold this book, the urn of ashes,
'Tis my true love's sepulchre.

IV

I DREAMT that I was God Himself
Whom heavenly joy immerses,
And all the angels sat about
And praised my verses.

V

THE mutilated choir boys
When I begin to sing
Complain about the awful noise
And call my voice too thick a thing.

When light their voices lift them up,
Bright notes against the ear,
Through trills and runs like crystal,
Ring delicate and clear.

They sing of Love that's grown desirous,
Of Love, and joy that is Love's inmost part,
And all the ladies swim through tears
Toward such a work of art.

VI

THIS delightful young man
Should not lack for honourers,
He propitiates me with oysters,
With Rhine wine and liqueurs.

How his coat and pants adorn him!
Yet his ties are more adorning,
In these he daily comes to ask me:
"Are you feeling well this morning?"

He speaks of my extended fame,
My wit, charm, definitions,
And is diligent to serve me,
Is detailed in his provisions.

In evening company he sets his face
In most spirit*el* positions,
And declaims before the ladies
My *god-like* compositions.

O what comfort is it for me
To find him such, when the days bring
No comfort, at my time of life when
All good things go vanishing.

TRANSLATOR TO TRANSLATED

O Harry Heine, curses be,
I live too late to sup with thee!
Who can demolish at such polished ease
Philistia's pomp and Art's pomposities!

VII

SONG FROM "DIE HARZREISE"

I AM the Princess Ilza
In Ilsenstein I fare,
Come with me to that castle
And we'll be happy there.

Thy head will I cover over
With my waves' clarity
Till thou forget thy sorrow,
O wounded sorrowfully.

Thou wilt in my white arms there,
Nay, on my breast thou must
Forget and rest and dream there
For thine old legend-lust.

My lips and my heart are thine there
As they were his and mine.
His? Why the good King Harry's,
And he is dead lang syne.

Dead men stay alway dead men,
Life is the live man's part,
And I am fair and golden
With joy breathless at heart.

If my heart stay below there,
My crystal halls ring clear
To the dance of lords and ladies
In all their splendid gear.

The silken trains go rustling,
The spur-clinks sound between,
The dark dwarfs blow and bow there
Small horn and violin.

Yet shall my white arms hold thee,
That bound King Harry about.
Ah, I covered his ears with them
When the trumpet rang out.

VIII

NIGHT SONG

AND have you thoroughly kissed my lips?
  There was no particular haste,
And are you not ready when evening's come?
  There's no *particular* haste.

You've got the whole night before you,
  Heart's-all-belovèd-my-own;
In an uninterrupted night one can
  Get a good deal of kissing done.

THE HOUSE OF SPLENDOUR

'TIS Evanoe's,
A house not made with hands,
But out somewhere beyond the worldly ways
Her gold is spread, above, around, inwoven;
Strange ways and walls are fashioned out of it.

And I have seen my Lady in the sun,
Her hair was spread about, a sheaf of wings,
And red the sunlight was, behind it all.

And I have seen her there within her house,
With six great sapphires hung along the wall,
Low, panel-shaped, a-level with her knees,
And all her robe was woven of pale gold.

There are there many rooms and all of gold,
Of woven walls deep patterned, of email,
Of beaten work; and through the claret stone,
Set to some weaving, comes the aureate light.

Here am I come perforce my love of her,
Behold mine adoration
Maketh me clear, and there are powers in this
Which, played on by the virtues of her soul,
Break down the four-square walls of standing time.

THE FLAME

'TIS not a game that plays at mates and mating,
Provençe knew;
'Tis not a game of barter, lands and houses,
Provençe knew.
We who are wise beyond your dream of wisdom,
Drink our immortal moments; we "pass through."
We have gone forth beyond your bonds and borders,
Provençe knew;
And all the tales of Oisin say but this:
That man doth pass the net of days and hours.
Where time is shrivelled down to time's seed corn
We of the Ever-living, in that light
Meet through our veils and whisper, and of love.

O smoke and shadow of a darkling world,
These, and the rest, and all the rest we knew.

'Tis not a game that plays at mates and mating,
'Tis not a game of barter, lands and houses,
'Tis not "of days and nights" and troubling years,
Of cheeks grown sunken and glad hair gone gray;
There *is* the subtler music, the clear light
Where time burns back about th' eternal embers.
We are not shut from all the thousand heavens:
Lo, there are many gods whom we have seen,
Folk of unearthly fashion, places splendid,
Bulwarks of beryl and of chrysoprase.

Sapphire Benacus, in thy mists and thee
Nature herself's turned metaphysical,
Who can look on that blue and not believe?

Thou hooded opal, thou eternal pearl,
O thou dark secret with a shimmering floor,
Through all thy various mood I know thee mine;

If I have merged my soul, or utterly
Am solved and bound in, through aught here on earth,
There canst thou find me, O thou anxious thou,
Who call'st about my gates for some lost me;
I say my soul flowed back, became translucent.
Search not my lips, O Love, let go my hands,
This thing that moves as man is no more mortal.
If thou hast seen my shade sans character,
If thou hast seen that mirror of all moments,
That glass to all things that o'ershadow it,
Call not that mirror me, for I have slipped
Your grasp, I have eluded.

HORAE BEATAE INSCRIPTIO

HOW will this beauty, when I am far hence,
Sweep back upon me and engulf my mind!

How will these hours, when we twain are gray,
Turned in their sapphire tide, come flooding o'er us!

THE ALTAR

LET us build here an exquisite friendship,
The flame, the autumn, and the green rose of love
Fought out their strife here, 'tis a place of wonder;
Where these have been, meet 'tis, the ground is holy.

AU SALON

Her grave, sweet haughtiness
Pleaseth me, and in like wise
Her quiet ironies.
Others are beautiful, none more, some less.

I SUPPOSE, when poetry comes down to facts,
When our souls are returned to the gods

And the spheres they belong in,
Here in the every-day where our acts
Rise up and judge us;

I suppose there are a few dozen verities
That no shift of mood can shake from us:

One place where we'd rather have tea
(Thus far hath modernity brought us)
"Tea" (Damn you!)

Have tea, damn the Caesars,
Talk of the latest success, give wing to some scandal,
Garble a name we detest, and for prejudice?
Set loose the whole consummate pack

to bay like Sir Roger de Coverley's

This our reward for our works,
sic crescit gloria mundi:
Some circle of not more than three
that we prefer to play up to,
Some few whom we'd rather please
than hear the whole aegrum vulgus
Splitting its beery jowl
a-meaowling our praises.

Some certain peculiar things,
cari laresque, penates,
Some certain accustomed forms,
the absolute unimportant.

AU JARDIN

O YOU away high there,
                    you that lean
From amber lattices upon the cobalt night,
I am below amid the pine trees,
Amid the little pine trees, hear me!

"The jester walked in the garden."
                            Did he so?
Well, there's no use your loving me
That way, Lady;
For I've nothing but songs to give you.

I am set wide upon the world's ways
To say that life is, some way, a gay thing,
But you never string two days upon one wire
But there'll come sorrow of it.
                    And I loved a love once,
Over beyond the moon there,
                I loved a love once,
And, may be, more times,

But she danced like a pink moth in the shrubbery.

Oh, I know you women from the "other folk,"
And it'll all come right,
O' Sundays.

"The jester walked in the garden."
                    Did he so?

RIPOSTES
(1912)

To
WILLIAM CARLOS WILLIAMS

"Quos ego Persephonae maxima dona feram."
PROPERTIUS

SILET

WHEN I behold how black, immortal ink
Drips from my deathless pen—ah, well-away!
Why should we stop at all for what I think?
There is enough in what I chance to say.

It is enough that we once came together;
What is the use of setting it to rime?
When it is autumn do we get spring weather,
Or gather may of harsh northwindish time?

It is enough that we once came together;
What if the wind have turned against the rain?
It is enough that we once came together;
Time has seen this, and will not turn again;

And who are we, who know that last intent,
To plague to-morrow with a testament!

Verona 1911

IN EXITUM CUIUSDAM

On a certain one's departure

"TIME'S bitter flood"! Oh, that's all very well,
But where's the old friend hasn't fallen off,
Or slacked his hand-grip when you first gripped fame?
I know your circle and can fairly tell
What you have kept and what you've left behind:
I know my circle and know very well
How many faces I'd have out of mind.

THE TOMB AT AKR ÇAAR

"I AM thy soul, Nikoptis.   I have watched
These five millennia, and thy dead eyes
Moved not, nor ever answer my desire,
And thy light limbs, wherethrough I leapt aflame,
Burn not with me nor any saffron thing.

See, the light grass sprang up to pillow thee,
And kissed thee with a myriad grassy tongues;
But not thou me.
I have read out the gold upon the wall,
And wearied out my thought upon the signs.
And there is no new thing in all this place.

I have been kind.   See, I have left the jars sealed,
Lest thou shouldst wake and whimper for thy wine.
And all thy robes I have kept smooth on thee.

O thou unmindful!   How should I forget!
—Even the river many days ago,
The river? thou wast over young.
And three souls came upon Thee—
And I came.
And I flowed in upon thee, beat them off;
I have been intimate with thee, known thy ways.
Have I not touched thy palms and finger-tips,
Flowed in, and through thee and about thy heels?
How 'came I in'?   Was I not thee and Thee?

And no sun comes to rest me in this place,
And I am torn against the jagged dark,
And no light beats upon me, and you say
No word, day after day.

Oh!   I could get me out, despite the marks
And all their crafty work upon the door,
Out through the glass-green fields. . . .
. . . .
Yet it is quiet here:
I do not go."

PORTRAIT D'UNE FEMME

YOUR mind and you are our Sargasso Sea,
London has swept about you this score years
And bright ships left you this or that in fee:
Ideas, old gossip, oddments of all things,
Strange spars of knowledge and dimmed wares of price.
Great minds have sought you—lacking someone else.
You have been second always. Tragical?
No. You preferred it to the usual thing:
One dull man, dulling and uxorious,
One average mind—with one thought less, each year.
Oh, you are patient, I have seen you sit
Hours, where something might have floated up.
And now you pay one. Yes, you richly pay.
You are a person of some interest, one comes to you
And takes strange gain away:
Trophies fished up; some curious suggestion;
Fact that leads nowhere; and a tale or two,
Pregnant with mandrakes, or with something else
That might prove useful and yet never proves,
That never fits a corner or shows use,
Or finds its hour upon the loom of days:
The tarnished, gaudy, wonderful old work;
Idols and ambergris and rare inlays,
These are your riches, your great store; and yet
For all this sea-hoard of deciduous things,
Strange woods half sodden, and new brighter stuff:
In the slow float of differing light and deep,
No! there is nothing! In the whole and all,
Nothing that's quite your own.
           Yet this is you.

N.Y.

MY City, my beloved, my white!   Ah, slender,
Listen!   Listen to me, and I will breathe into thee a soul.
Delicately upon the reed, attend me!

Now do I know that I am mad,
For here are a million people surly with traffic;
This is no maid.
Neither could I play upon any reed if I had one.

My City, my beloved,
Thou art a maid with no breasts,
Thou art slender as a silver reed.
Listen to me, attend me!
And I will breathe into thee a soul,
And thou shalt live for ever.

A GIRL

THE tree has entered my hands,
The sap has ascended my arms,
The tree has grown in my breast—
Downward,
The branches grow out of me, like arms.

Tree you are,
Moss you are,
You are violets with wind above them.
A child—*so* high—you are,
And all this is folly to the world.

"PHASELLUS ILLE"

THIS *papier-mâché*, which you see, my friends,
Saith 'twas the worthiest of editors.
Its mind was made up in "the seventies,"
Nor hath it ever since changed that concoction.
It works to represent that school of thought
Which brought the hair-cloth chair to such perfection,
Nor will the horrid threats of Bernard Shaw
Shake up the stagnant pool of its convictions;
Nay, should the deathless voice of all the world
Speak once again for its sole stimulation,
'Twould not move it one jot from left to right.

Come Beauty barefoot from the Cyclades,
She'd find a model for St. Anthony
In this thing's sure *decorum* and behaviour.

AN OBJECT

THIS thing, that hath a code and not a core,
Hath set acquaintance where might be affections,
And nothing now
      Disturbeth his reflections.

QUIES

THIS is another of our ancient loves.
Pass and be silent, Rullus, for the day
Hath lacked a something since this lady passed;
Hath lacked a something. 'Twas but marginal.

THE SEAFARER

FROM THE ANGLO-SAXON

MAY I for my own self song's truth reckon,
Journey's jargon, how I in harsh days
Hardship endured oft.
Bitter breast-cares have I abided,
Known on my keel many a care's hold,
And dire sea-surge, and there I oft spent
Narrow nightwatch nigh the ship's head
While she tossed close to cliffs.   Coldly afflicted,
My feet were by frost benumbed.
Chill its chains are; chafing sighs
Hew my heart round and hunger begot
Mere-weary mood.   Lest man know not
That he on dry land loveliest liveth,
List how I, care-wretched, on ice-cold sea,
Weathered the winter, wretched outcast
Deprived of my kinsmen;
Hung with hard ice-flakes, where hail-scur flew,
There I heard naught save the harsh sea
And ice-cold wave, at whiles the swan cries,
Did for my games the gannet's clamour,
Sea-fowls' loudness was for me laughter,
The mews' singing all my mead-drink.
Storms, on the stone-cliffs beaten, fell on the stern
In icy feathers; full oft the eagle screamed
With spray on his pinion.
                              Not any protector
May make merry man faring needy.
This he little believes, who aye in winsome life
Abides 'mid burghers some heavy business,
Wealthy and wine-flushed, how I weary oft
Must bide above brine.
Neareth nightshade, snoweth from north,
Frost froze the land, hail fell on earth then,
Corn of the coldest.   Nathless there knocketh now
The heart's thought that I on high streams

: 62 :

The salt-wavy tumult traverse alone.
Moaneth alway my mind's lust
That I fare forth, that I afar hence
Seek out a foreign fastness.
For this there's no mood-lofty man over earth's midst,
Not though he be given his good, but will have in his youth greed;
Nor his deed to the daring, nor his king to the faithful
But shall have his sorrow for sea-fare
Whatever his lord will.
He hath not heart for harping, nor in ring-having
Nor winsomeness to wife, nor world's delight
Nor any whit else save the wave's slash,
Yet longing comes upon him to fare forth on the water.
Bosque taketh blossom, cometh beauty of berries,
Fields to fairness, land fares brisker,
All this admonisheth man eager of mood,
The heart turns to travel so that he then thinks
On flood-ways to be far departing.
Cuckoo calleth with gloomy crying,
He singeth summerward, bodeth sorrow,
The bitter heart's blood.   Burgher knows not—
He the prosperous man—what some perform
Where wandering them widest draweth.
So that but now my heart burst from my breastlock,
My mood 'mid the mere-flood,
Over the whale's acre, would wander wide.
On earth's shelter cometh oft to me,
Eager and ready, the crying lone-flyer,
Whets for the whale-path the heart irresistibly,
O'er tracks of ocean; seeing that anyhow
My lord deems to me this dead life
On loan and on land, I believe not
That any earth-weal eternal standeth
Save there be somewhat calamitous
That, ere a man's tide go, turn it to twain.
Disease or oldness or sword-hate
Beats out the breath from doom-gripped body.
And for this, every earl whatever, for those speaking after—

Laud of the living, boasteth some last word,
That he will work ere he pass onward,
Frame on the fair earth 'gainst foes his malice,
Daring ado, . . .
So that all men shall honour him after
And his laud beyond them remain 'mid the English,
Aye, for ever, a lasting life's-blast,
Delight 'mid the doughty.
                                    Days little durable,
And all arrogance of earthen riches,
There come now no kings nor Cæsars
Nor gold-giving lords like those gone.
Howe'er in mirth most magnified,
Whoe'er lived in life most lordliest,
Drear all this excellence, delights undurable!
Waneth the watch, but the world holdeth.
Tomb hideth trouble.   The blade is layed low.
Earthly glory ageth and seareth.
No man at all going the earth's gait,
But age fares against him, his face paleth,
Grey-haired he groaneth, knows gone companions,
Lordly men, are to earth o'ergiven,
Nor may he then the flesh-cover, whose life ceaseth,
Nor eat the sweet nor feel the sorry,
Nor stir hand nor think in mid heart,
And though he strew the grave with gold,
His born brothers, their buried bodies
Be an unlikely treasure hoard.

THE CLOAK*

THOU keep'st thy rose-leaf
　　Till the rose-time will be over,
Think'st thou that Death will kiss thee?
Think'st thou that the Dark House
　　Will find thee such a lover
As I?　Will the new roses miss thee?

Prefer my cloak unto the cloak of dust
　　'Neath which the last year lies,
For thou shouldst more mistrust
　　Time than my eyes.

* Asclepiades, Julianus Ægyptus.

Δώρια

BE in me as the eternal moods of the bleak wind, and not
As transient things are—
　　gaiety of flowers.
Have me in the strong loneliness
　　of sunless cliffs
And of grey waters.
　　Let the gods speak softly of us
In days hereafter,
　　The shadowy flowers of Orcus
Remember thee.

APPARUIT

GOLDEN rose the house, in the portal I saw
thee, a marvel, carven in subtle stuff, a
portent.   Life died down in the lamp and flickered,
          caught at the wonder.

Crimson, frosty with dew, the roses bend where
thou afar, moving in the glamorous sun,
drinkst in life of earth, of the air, the tissue
          golden about thee.

Green the ways, the breath of the fields is thine there,
open lies the land, yet the steely going
darkly hast thou dared and the dreaded æther
          parted before thee.

Swift at courage thou in the shell of gold, casting a-loose the cloak of the body, camest
straight, then shone thine oriel and the stunned light
          faded about thee.

Half the graven shoulder, the throat aflash with
strands of light inwoven about it, loveliest of all things, frail alabaster, ah me!
          swift in departing.

Clothed in goldish weft, delicately perfect,
gone as wind!   The cloth of the magical hands!
Thou a slight thing, thou in access of cunning
          dar'dst to assume this?

THE NEEDLE

COME, or the stellar tide will slip away.
Eastward avoid the hour of its decline,
Now! for the needle trembles in my soul!

Here have we had our vantage, the good hour.
Here we have had our day, your day and mine.
Come now, before this power
That bears us up, shall turn against the pole.

Mock not the flood of stars, the thing's to be.
O Love, come now, this land turns evil slowly.
The waves bore in, soon will they bear away.

The treasure is ours, make we fast land with it.
Move we and take the tide, with its next favour,
Abide
Under some neutral force
Until this course turneth aside.

SUB MARE

IT is, and is not, I am sane enough,
Since you have come this place has hovered round me,
This fabrication built of autumn roses,
Then there's a goldish colour, different.

And one gropes in these things as delicate
Algæ reach up and out, beneath
Pale slow green surgings of the underwave,
'Mid these things older than the names they have,
These things that are familiars of the god.

THE PLUNGE

I WOULD bathe myself in strangeness:
These comforts heaped upon me, smother me!
I burn, I scald so for the new,
New friends, new faces,
Places!
Oh to be out of this,
This that is all I wanted
            —save the new.

And you,
Love, you the much, the more desired!
Do I not loathe all walls, streets, stones,
All mire, mist, all fog,
All ways of traffic?
You, I would have flow over me like water,
Oh, but far out of this!
Grass, and low fields, and hills,
And sun,
Oh, sun enough!
Out, and alone, among some
Alien people!

A VIRGINAL

NO, no! Go from me. I have left her lately.
I will not spoil my sheath with lesser brightness,
For my surrounding air hath a new lightness;
Slight are her arms, yet they have bound me straitly
And left me cloaked as with a gauze of æther;
As with sweet leaves; as with subtle clearness.
Oh, I have picked up magic in her nearness
To sheathe me half in half the things that sheathe her.
No, no! Go from me. I have still the flavour,
Soft as spring wind that's come from birchen bowers.
Green come the shoots, aye April in the branches,
As winter's wound with her sleight hand she staunches,
Hath of the trees a likeness of the savour:
As white their bark, so white this lady's hours.

PAN IS DEAD

"PAN is dead. Great Pan is dead.
    Ah! bow your heads, ye maidens all,
    And weave ye him his coronal."

*   "There is no summer in the leaves,*
And withered are the sedges;
*   How shall we weave a coronal,*
Or gather floral pledges?"

"That I may not say, Ladies.
Death was ever a churl.
That I may not say, Ladies.
How should he show a reason,
That he has taken our Lord away
Upon such hollow season?"

DIEU! QU'IL LA FAIT

From Charles d'Orléans

GOD! that mad'st her well regard her,
How she is so fair and bonny;
For the great charms that are upon her
Ready are all folks to reward her.

Who could part him from her borders
When spells are alway renewed on her?
God! that mad'st her well regard her,
How she is so fair and bonny.

From here to there to the sea's border,
Dame nor damsel there's not any
Hath of perfect charms so many.
Thoughts of her are of dream's order:
God! that mad'st her well regard her.

THE PICTURE*

THE eyes of this dead lady speak to me,
For here was love, was not to be drowned out.
And here desire, not to be kissed away.
The eyes of this dead lady speak to me.

* *Venus Reclining*, by Jacopo del Sellaio (1442–1493).

OF JACOPO DEL SELLAIO

THIS man knew out the secret ways of love,
No man could paint such things who did not know.
And now she's gone, who was his Cyprian,
And you are here, who are "The Isles" to me.

And here's the thing that lasts the whole thing out:
The eyes of this dead lady speak to me.

THE RETURN

SEE, they return; ah, see the tentative
Movements, and the slow feet,
The trouble in the pace and the uncertain
            Wavering!

See, they return, one, and by one,
With fear, as half-awakened;
As if the snow should hesitate
And murmur in the wind,
            and half turn back;
These were the "Wing'd-with-Awe,"
            Inviolable.

Gods of the wingèd shoe!
With them the silver hounds,
            sniffing the trace of air!

Haie! Haie!
        These were the swift to harry;
These the keen-scented;
These were the souls of blood.

Slow on the leash,
            pallid the leash-men!

THE ALCHEMIST

Chant for the Transmutation of Metals

SAÎL of Claustra, Aelis, Azalais,
As you move among the bright trees;
As your voices, under the larches of Paradise
Make a clear sound,
Saîl of Claustra, Aelis, Azalais,
Raimona, Tibors, Berangèrë,
'Neath the dark gleam of the sky;
Under night, the peacock-throated,
Bring the saffron-coloured shell,
Bring the red gold of the maple,
Bring the light of the birch tree in autumn
Mirals, Cembelins, Audiarda,

                                        Remember this fire.

Elain, Tireis, Alcmena
'Mid the silver rustling of wheat,
Agradiva, Anhes, Ardenca,
From the plum-coloured lake, in stillness,
From the molten dyes of the water
Bring the burnished nature of fire;
Briseis, Lianor, Loica,
From the wide earth and the olive,
From the poplars weeping their amber,
By the bright flame of the fishing torch

                                        Remember this fire.

Midonz, with the gold of the sun, the leaf of the poplar, by the
    light of the amber,
Midonz, daughter of the sun, shaft of the tree, silver of the leaf,
    light of the yellow of the amber,
Midonz, gift of the God, gift of the light, gift of the amber of the
    sun,

                                  Give light to the metal.

Anhes of Rocacoart, Ardenca, Aemelis,
From the power of grass,
From the white, alive in the seed,
From the heat of the bud,

From the copper of the leaf in autumn,
From the bronze of the maple, from the sap in the bough;
Lianor, Ioanna, Loica,
By the stir of the fin,
By the trout asleep in the gray-green of water;
Vanna, Mandetta, Viera, Alodetta, Picarda, Manuela
From the red gleam of copper,
Ysaut, Ydone, slight rustling of leaves,
Vierna, Jocelynn, daring of spirits,
By the mirror of burnished copper,
       O Queen of Cypress,
Out of Erebus, the flat-lying breath,
Breath that is stretched out beneath the world:
Out of Erebus, out of the flat waste of air, lying beneath the world;
Out of the brown leaf-brown colourless
       Bring the imperceptible cool.
Elain, Tireis, Alcmena,
       Quiet this metal!
Let the manes put off their terror, let them put off their aqueous
  bodies with fire.
Let them assume the milk-white bodies of agate.
Let them draw together the bones of the metal.

Selvaggia, Guiscarda, Mandetta,
       Rain flakes of gold on the water
Azure and flaking silver of water,
Alcyon, Phætona, Alcmena,
Pallor of silver, pale lustre of Latona,
By these, from the malevolence of the dew
       Guard this alembic.
Elain, Tireis, Alodetta
       Quiet this metal.

LUSTRA

DEFINITION: LUSTRUM: an offering for the sins of the whole people, made by the censors at the expiration of their five years of office, etc. Elementary Latin Dictionary of Charlton T. Lewis.

Vail de Lencour
Cui dono lepidum novum libellum.

And the days are not full enough
And the nights are not full enough
And life slips by like a field mouse
   Not shaking the grass.

TENZONE

WILL people accept them?
    (i.e. these songs).
As a timorous wench from a centaur
    (or a centurion),
Already they flee, howling in terror.

Will they be touched with the verisimilitudes?
    Their virgin stupidity is untemptable.
I beg you, my friendly critics,
Do not set about to procure me an audience.

I mate with my free kind upon the crags;
    the hidden recesses
Have heard the echo of my heels,
    in the cool light,
    in the darkness.

THE CONDOLENCE

A mis soledades voy,
De mis soledades vengo,
Porque por andar conmigo
Mi bastan mis pensamientos.
LOPE DE VEGA

O MY fellow sufferers, songs of my youth,
A lot of asses praise you because you are "virile,"
We, you, I! We are "Red Bloods"!
Imagine it, my fellow sufferers—
Our maleness lifts us out of the ruck,
    Who'd have foreseen it?

O my fellow sufferers, we went out under the trees,
We were in especial bored with male stupidity.
We went forth gathering delicate thoughts,
Our "*fantastikon*" delighted to serve us.
We were not exasperated with women,
    for the female is ductile.

And now you hear what is said to us:
We are compared to that sort of person
Who wanders about announcing his sex
As if he had just discovered it.
Let us leave this matter, my songs,
          and return to that which concerns us.

THE GARRET

COME, let us pity those who are better off than we are.
Come, my friend, and remember
          that the rich have butlers and no friends,
And we have friends and no butlers.
Come, let us pity the married and the unmarried.

Dawn enters with little feet
          like a gilded Pavlova,
And I am near my desire.
Nor has life in it aught better
Than this hour of clear coolness,
          the hour of waking together.

THE GARDEN

En robe de parade.
SAMAIN

LIKE a skein of loose silk blown against a wall
She walks by the railing of a path in Kensington Gardens,
And she is dying piece-meal
          of a sort of emotional anæmia.

And round about there is a rabble
Of the filthy, sturdy, unkillable infants of the very poor.
They shall inherit the earth.

In her is the end of breeding.
Her boredom is exquisite and excessive.

She would like some one to speak to her,
And is almost afraid that I
    will commit that indiscretion.

ORTUS

HOW have I laboured?
How have I not laboured
To bring her soul to birth,
To give these elements a name and a centre!
She is beautiful as the sunlight, and as fluid.
She has no name, and no place.
How have I laboured to bring her soul into separation;
To give her a name and her being!

Surely you are bound and entwined,
You are mingled with the elements unborn;
I have loved a stream and a shadow.

I beseech you enter your life.
I beseech you learn to say "I,"
When I question you;
For you are no part, but a whole,
No portion, but a being.

SALUTATION

O GENERATION of the thoroughly smug
    and thoroughly uncomfortable,
I have seen fishermen picnicking in the sun,
I have seen them with untidy families,
I have seen their smiles full of teeth
    and heard ungainly laughter.
And I am happier than you are,
And they were happier than I am;
And the fish swim in the lake
    and do not even own clothing.

SALUTATION THE SECOND

YOU were praised, my books,
      because I had just come from the country;
I was twenty years behind the times
      so you found an audience ready.
I do not disown you,
      do not you disown your progeny.

Here they stand without quaint devices,
Here they are with nothing archaic about them.
Observe the irritation in general:

"Is this," they say, "the nonsense
      that we expect of poets?"
"Where is the Picturesque?"
      "Where is the vertigo of emotion?"
"No! his first work was the best."
      "Poor Dear! he has lost his illusions."

Go, little naked and impudent songs,
Go with a light foot!
(Or with two light feet, if it please you!)
Go and dance shamelessly!
Go with an impertinent frolic!

Greet the grave and the stodgy,
Salute them with your thumbs at your noses.

Here are your bells and confetti.
Go! rejuvenate things!
Rejuvenate even "The Spectator."
      Go! and make cat calls!
Dance and make people blush,
Dance the dance of the phallus
      and tell anecdotes of Cybele!
Speak of the indecorous conduct of the Gods!
      (Tell it to Mr. Strachey)

Ruffle the skirts of prudes,
      speak of their knees and ankles.

But, above all, go to practical people—
      go! jangle their door-bells!
Say that you do no work
      and that you will live forever.

THE SPRING

Ἦρι μὲν αἴ τε κυδώνιαι
IBYCUS

  CYDONIAN Spring with her attendant train,
Maelids and water-girls,
Stepping beneath a boisterous wind from Thrace,
Throughout this sylvan place
Spreads the bright tips,
And every vine-stock is
Clad in new brilliancies.
                And wild desire
Falls like black lightning.
O bewildered heart,
Though every branch have back what last year lost,
She, who moved here amid the cyclamen,
Moves only now a clinging tenuous ghost.

ALBATRE

THIS lady in the white bath-robe which she calls a peignoir,
Is, for the time being, the mistress of my friend,
And the delicate white feet of her little white dog
Are not more delicate than she is,
Nor would Gautier himself have despised their contrasts in
      whiteness
As she sits in the great chair
Between the two indolent candles.

CAUSA

I JOIN these words for four people,
Some others may overhear them,
O world, I am sorry for you,
You do not know these four people.

COMMISSION

GO, my songs, to the lonely and the unsatisfied,
Go also to the nerve-wracked, go to the enslaved-by-convention,
Bear to them my contempt for their oppressors.
Go as a great wave of cool water,
Bear my contempt of oppressors.

Speak against unconscious oppression,
Speak against the tyranny of the unimaginative,
Speak against bonds.
Go to the bourgeoise who is dying of her ennuis,
Go to the women in suburbs.
Go to the hideously wedded,
Go to them whose failure is concealed,
Go to the unluckily mated,
Go to the bought wife,
Go to the woman entailed.

Go to those who have delicate lust,
Go to those whose delicate desires are thwarted,
Go like a blight upon the dulness of the world;
Go with your edge against this,
Strengthen the subtle cords,
Bring confidence upon the algæ and the tentacles of the soul.

Go in a friendly manner,
Go with an open speech.
Be eager to find new evils and new good,
Be against all forms of oppression.
Go to those who are thickened with middle age,
To those who have lost their interest.

Go to the adolescent who are smothered in family—
Oh how hideous it is
To see three generations of one house gathered together!
It is like an old tree with shoots,
And with some branches rotted and falling.

Go out and defy opinion,
Go against this vegetable bondage of the blood.
Be against all sorts of mortmain.

A PACT

I MAKE a pact with you, Walt Whitman—
I have detested you long enough.
I come to you as a grown child
Who has had a pig-headed father;
I am old enough now to make friends.
It was you that broke the new wood,
Now is a time for carving.
We have one sap and one root—
Let there be commerce between us.

SURGIT FAMA

THERE is a truce among the gods,
Korè is seen in the North
Skirting the blue-gray sea
In gilded and russet mantle.
The corn has again its mother and she, Leuconoë,
That failed never women,
Fails not the earth now.

The tricksome Hermes is here;
He moves behind me
Eager to catch my words,
Eager to spread them with rumour;
To set upon them his change

: 83 :

Crafty and subtle;
To alter them to his purpose;
But do thou speak true, even to the letter:

"Once more in Delos, once more is the altar a-quiver.
Once more is the chant heard.
Once more are the never abandoned gardens
Full of gossip and old tales."

DANCE FIGURE

For the Marriage in Cana of Galilee

DARK eyed,
O woman of my dreams,
Ivory sandaled,
There is none like thee among the dancers,
None with swift feet.

I have not found thee in the tents,
In the broken darkness.
I have not found thee at the well-head
Among the women with pitchers.

Thine arms are as a young sapling under the bark;
Thy face as a river with lights.

White as an almond are thy shoulders;
As new almonds stripped from the husk.
They guard thee not with eunuchs;
Not with bars of copper.

Gilt turquoise and silver are in the place of thy rest.
A brown robe, with threads of gold woven in patterns, hast thou
    gathered about thee,
O Nathat-Ikanaie, "Tree-at-the-river."

As a rillet among the sedge are thy hands upon me;
Thy fingers a frosted stream.

Thy maidens are white like pebbles;
Their music about thee!

There is none like thee among the dancers;
None with swift feet.

APRIL

Nympharum membra disjecta

THREE spirits came to me
And drew me apart
To where the olive boughs
Lay stripped upon the ground:
Pale carnage beneath bright mist.

GENTILDONNA

SHE passed and left no quiver in the veins, who now
Moving among the trees, and clinging
                    in the air she severed,
Fanning the grass she walked on then, endures:

Grey olive leaves beneath a rain-cold sky.

THE REST

O HELPLESS few in my country,
O remnant enslaved!

Artists broken against her,
A-stray, lost in the villages,
Mistrusted, spoken-against,

Lovers of beauty, starved,
Thwarted with systems,
Helpless against the control;

You who can not wear yourselves out
By persisting to successes,
You who can only speak,
Who can not steel yourselves into reiteration;

You of the finer sense,
Broken against false knowledge,
You who can know at first hand,
Hated, shut in, mistrusted:

Take thought:
I have weathered the storm,
I have beaten out my exile.

LES MILLWIN

THE little Millwins attend the Russian Ballet.
The mauve and greenish souls of the little Millwins
Were seen lying along the upper seats
Like so many unused boas.

The turbulent and undisciplined host of art students—
The rigorous deputation from "Slade"—
Was before them.

With arms exalted, with fore-arms
Crossed in great futuristic X's, the art students
Exulted, they beheld the splendours of *Cleopatra*.

And the little Millwins beheld these things;
With their large and anæmic eyes they looked out upon this
    configuration.

Let us therefore mention the fact,
For it seems to us worthy of record.

FURTHER INSTRUCTIONS

COME, my songs, let us express our baser passions,
Let us express our envy of the man with a steady job and no worry
    about the future.
You are very idle, my songs.
I fear you will come to a bad end.
You stand about in the streets,
You loiter at the corners and bus-stops,
You do next to nothing at all.

You do not even express our inner nobilities,
You will come to a very bad end.

And I?
I have gone half cracked,
I have talked to you so much that
                           I almost see you about me,
Insolent little beasts, shameless, devoid of clothing!

But you, newest song of the lot,
You are not old enough to have done much mischief,
I will get you a green coat out of China
With dragons worked upon it,
I will get you the scarlet silk trousers
From the statue of the infant Christ in Santa Maria Novella,
Lest they say we are lacking in taste,
Or that there is no caste in this family.

A SONG OF THE DEGREES

I

REST me with Chinese colours,
For I think the glass is evil.

II

The wind moves above the wheat—
With a silver crashing,
A thin war of metal.

I have known the golden disc,
I have seen it melting above me.
I have known the stone-bright place,
        The hall of clear colours.

III

O glass subtly evil, O confusion of colours!
O light bound and bent in, O soul of the captive,
Why am I warned?   Why am I sent away?
Why is your glitter full of curious mistrust?
O glass subtle and cunning, O powdery gold!
O filaments of amber, two-faced iridescence!

ITÉ

GO, my songs, seek your praise from the young
        and from the intolerant,
Move among the lovers of perfection alone.
Seek ever to stand in the hard Sophoclean light
And take your wounds from it gladly.

DUM CAPITOLIUM SCANDET

HOW many will come after me
    singing as well as I sing, none better;
Telling the heart of their truth
    as I have taught them to tell it;
Fruit of my seed,
    O my unnameable children.
Know then that I loved you from afore-time,
Clear speakers, naked in the sun, untrammelled.

Τὸ Καλόν

Even in my dreams you have denied yourself to me
And sent me only your handmaids.

THE STUDY IN AESTHETICS

THE very small children in patched clothing,
Being smitten with an unusual wisdom,
Stopped in their play as she passed them
And cried up from their cobbles:

    Guarda! Ahi, guarda! ch' è be'a!*

But three years after this
I heard the young Dante, whose last name I do not know—
For there are, in Sirmione, twenty-eight young Dantes and
    thirty-four Catulli;
And there had been a great catch of sardines,
And his elders
Were packing them in the great wooden boxes
For the market in Brescia, and he
Leapt about, snatching at the bright fish

---

* *Bella.*

And getting in both of their ways;
And in vain they commanded him to *sta fermo!*
And when they would not let him arrange
The fish in the boxes
He stroked those which were already arranged,
Murmuring for his own satisfaction
This identical phrase:

Ch' è be'a.

And at this I was mildly abashed.

THE BELLAIRES

Aus meinen grossen Schmerzen
Mach' ich die kleinen Lieder

THE good Bellaires
Do not understand the conduct of this world's affairs.
In fact they understood them so badly
That they have had to cross the Channel.
Nine lawyers, four counsels, five judges and three proctors of the
    King,
Together with the respective wives, husbands, sisters and
    heterogeneous connections of the good Bellaires,
Met to discuss their affairs;
But the good Bellaires have so little understood their affairs
That now there is no one at all
Who can understand any affair of theirs.   Yet
Fourteen hunters still eat in the stables of
The good Squire Bellaire;
But these may not suffer attainder,
For they may not belong to the good Squire Bellaire
But to his wife.
On the contrary, if they do not belong to his wife,
He will plead
A "freedom from attainder"
For twelve horses and also for twelve boarhounds

From Charles the Fourth;
And a further freedom for the remainder
Of horses, from Henry the Fourth.
But the judges,
Being free of mediæval scholarship,
Will pay no attention to this,
And there will be only the more confusion,
Replevin, estoppel, espavin and what not.

Nine lawyers, four counsels, etc.,
Met to discuss their affairs,
But the sole result was bills
From lawyers to whom no one was indebted,
And even the lawyers
Were uncertain who was supposed to be indebted to them.

Wherefore the good Squire Bellaire
Resides now at Agde and Biaucaire.
To Carcassonne, Pui, and Alais
He fareth from day to day,
Or takes the sea air
Between Marseilles
And Beziers.
And for all this I have considerable regret,
For the good Bellaires
Are very charming people.

THE NEW CAKE OF SOAP

LO, how it gleams and glistens in the sun
Like the cheek of a Chesterton.

SALVATIONISTS

I

COME, my songs, let us speak of perfection—
We shall get ourselves rather disliked.

II

Ah yes, my songs, let us resurrect
The very excellent term *Rusticus*.
Let us apply it in all its opprobrium
To those to whom it applies.
And you may decline to make them immortal,
For we shall consider them and their state
In delicate
Opulent silence.

III

Come, my songs,
Let us take arms against this sea of stupidities—
Beginning with Mumpodorus;
And against this sea of vulgarities—
Beginning with Nimmim;
And against this sea of imbeciles—
All the Bulmenian literati.

EPITAPH

LEUCIS, who intended a Grand Passion,
Ends with a willingness-to-oblige.

ARIDES

THE bashful Arides
Has married an ugly wife,
He was bored with his manner of life,
Indifferent and discouraged he thought he might as
Well do this as anything else.

Saying within his heart, "I am no use to myself,
"Let her, if she wants me, take me."
He went to his doom.

THE BATH TUB

AS a bathtub lined with white porcelain,
When the hot water gives out or goes tepid,
So is the slow cooling of our chivalrous passion,
O my much praised but-not-altogether-satisfactory lady.

THE TEMPERAMENTS

NINE adulteries, 12 liaisons, 64 fornications and something
    approaching a rape
Rest nightly upon the soul of our delicate friend Florialis,
And yet the man is so quiet and reserved in demeanour
That he passes for both bloodless and sexless.
Bastidides, on the contrary, who both talks and writes of nothing
    save copulation,
Has become the father of twins,
But he accomplished this feat at some cost;
He had to be four times cuckold.

AMITIES

Old friends the most.
W. B. Y.

I

To one, on returning certain years after.

YOU wore the same quite correct clothing,
You took no pleasure at all in my triumphs,
You had the same old air of condescension
Mingled with a curious fear
      That I, myself, might have enjoyed them.
Te Voilà, mon Bourrienne, you also shall be immortal.

II

To another.

And we say good-bye to you also,
For you seem never to have discovered
That your relationship is wholly parasitic;
Yet to our feasts you bring neither
Wit, nor good spirits, nor the pleasing attitudes
      Of discipleship.

III

But you, *bos amic*, we keep on,
For to you we owe a real debt:
In spite of your obvious flaws,
You once discovered a moderate chop-house.

IV

Iste fuit vir incultus,
Deo laus, quod est sepultus,
Vermes habent eius vultum
      A-a-a-a—A-men.

Ego autem jovialis
Gaudero contubernalis
Cum jocunda femina.

MEDITATIO

WHEN I carefully consider the curious habits of dogs
I am compelled to conclude
That man is the superior animal.

When I consider the curious habits of man
I confess, my friend, I am puzzled.

TO DIVES

WHO am I to condemn you, O Dives,
I who am as much embittered with poverty
As you are with useless riches?

LADIES

Agathas

FOUR and forty lovers had Agathas in the old days,
All of whom she refused;
And now she turns to me seeking love,
And her hair also is turning.

Young Lady

I have fed your lar with poppies,
I have adored you for three full years;
And now you grumble because your dress does not fit
And because I happen to say so.

Lesbia Illa

Memnon, Memnon, that lady
Who used to walk about amongst us
With such gracious uncertainty,
Is now wedded
To a British householder.
Lugete, Veneres! Lugete, Cupidinesque!

Flawless as Aphrodite,
Thoroughly beautiful,
Brainless,
The faint odour of your patchouli,
Faint, almost, as the lines of cruelty about your chin,
Assails me, and concerns me almost as little.

PHYLLIDULA

PHYLLIDULA is scrawny but amorous,
Thus have the gods awarded her,
That in pleasure she receives more than she can give;
If she does not count this blessed
Let her change her religion.

THE PATTERNS

ERINNA is a model parent,
Her children have never discovered her adulteries.
Lalage is also a model parent,
Her offspring are fat and happy.

CODA

O MY songs,
Why do you look so eagerly and so curiously into people's faces,
Will you find your lost dead among them?

THE SEEING EYE

THE small dogs look at the big dogs;
They observe unwieldly dimensions
And curious imperfections of odor.
Here is a formal male group:
The young men look upon their seniors,
They consider the elderly mind
And observe its inexplicable correlations.

Said Tsin-Tsu:
It is only in small dogs and the young
That we find minute observation.

ANCORA

GOOD God!   They say you are *risqué*, O canzonetti!
We who went out into the four A.M. of the world
Composing our albas,
We who shook off our dew with the rabbits,
We who have seen even Artemis a-binding her sandals,
Have we ever heard the like?
O mountains of Hellas!!
Gather about me, O Muses!
When we sat upon the granite brink in Helicon
Clothed in the tattered sunlight,
O Muses with delicate shins,
O Muses with delectable knee-joints,
When we splashed and were splashed with
The lucid Castalian spray,
Had we ever such an epithet cast upon us!!

"DOMPNA POIS DE ME NO'US CAL"

FROM THE PROVENÇAL OF EN BERTRANS DE BORN

LADY, since you care nothing for me,
And since you have shut me away from you
Causelessly,
I know not where to go seeking,
For certainly
I will never again gather
Joy so rich, and if I find not ever
A lady with look so speaking
To my desire, worth yours whom I have lost,
I'll have no other love at any cost.

And since I could not find a peer to you,
Neither one so fair, nor of such heart,
So eager and alert,
Nor with such art
In attire, nor so gay
Nor with gift so bountiful and so true,
I will go out a-searching,
Culling from each a fair trait
To make me a borrowed lady
Till I again find you ready.

Bels Cembelins, I take of you your colour,
For it's your own, and your glance
Where love is,
A proud thing I do here,
For, as to colour and eyes
I shall have missed nothing at all,
Having yours.
I ask of Midons Aelis (of Montfort)
Her straight speech free-running,
That my phantom lack not in cunning.

At Chalais of the Viscountess, I would
That she give me outright

Her two hands and her throat,
So take I my road
To Rochechouart,
Swift-foot to my Lady Anhes,
Seeing that Tristan's lady Iseutz had never
Such grace of locks, I do ye to wit,
Though she'd the far fame for it.

Of Audiart at Malemort,
Though she with a full heart
Wish me ill,
I'd have her form that's laced
So cunningly,
Without blemish, for her love
Breaks not nor turns aside.
I of Miels-de-ben demand
Her straight fresh body,
She is so supple and young,
Her robes can but do her wrong.

Her white teeth, of the Lady Faidita
I ask, and the fine courtesy
She hath to welcome one,
And such replies she lavishes
Within her nest;
Of Bels Mirals, the rest,
Tall stature and gaiety,
To make these avail
She knoweth well, betide
No change nor turning aside.

Ah, Bels Senher, Maent, at last
I ask naught from you,
Save that I have such hunger for
This phantom
As I've for you, such flame-lap,
And yet I'd rather
Ask of you than hold another,

Mayhap, right close and kissed.
Ah, lady, why have you cast
Me out, knowing you hold me so fast!

THE COMING OF WAR: ACTAEON

AN image of Lethe,
          and the fields
Full of faint light
          but golden,
Gray cliffs,
          and beneath them
A sea
Harsher than granite,
          unstill, never ceasing;
High forms
          with the movement of gods,
Perilous aspect;
          And one said:
"This is Actaeon."
          Actaeon of golden greaves!
Over fair meadows,
Over the cool face of that field,
Unstill, ever moving
Hosts of an ancient people,
The silent cortège.

AFTER CH'U YUAN

I WILL get me to the wood
Where the gods walk garlanded in wistaria,
By the silver blue flood
     move others with ivory cars.
There come forth many maidens
     to gather grapes for the leopards, my friend,
For there are leopards drawing the cars.

I will walk in the glade,
I will come out from the new thicket
    and accost the procession of maidens.
By Wu'-ti

LIU CH'E

THE rustling of the silk is discontinued,
Dust drifts over the court-yard,
There is no sound of foot-fall, and the leaves
Scurry into heaps and lie still,
And she the rejoicer of the heart is beneath them:

A wet leaf that clings to the threshold.

FAN-PIECE, FOR HER IMPERIAL LORD

    O FAN of white silk,
        clear as frost on the grass-blade,
    You also are laid aside.

TS'AI CHI'H

    THE petals fall in the fountain,
        the orange-coloured rose-leaves,
    Their ochre clings to the stone.

IN A STATION OF THE METRO

THE apparition of these faces in the crowd;
Petals on a wet, black bough.

ALBA

AS cool as the pale wet leaves
                          of lily-of-the-valley
She lay beside me in the dawn.

HEATHER

THE black panther treads at my side,
And above my fingers
There float the petal-like flames.

The milk-white girls
Unbend from the holly-trees,
And their snow-white leopard
Watches to follow our trace.

THE FAUN

HA! sir, I have seen you sniffing and snoozling about among my
                                          flowers.
And what, pray, do you know about horticulture, you capriped?
"Come, Auster, come Apeliota,
And see the faun in our garden.
But if you move or speak
This thing will run at you
And scare itself to spasms."

COITUS

THE gilded phaloi of the crocuses
                    are thrusting at the spring air.
Here is there naught of dead gods
But a procession of festival,
A procession, O Giulio Romano,
Fit for your spirit to dwell in.
Dione, your nights are upon us.

The dew is upon the leaf.
The night about us is restless.

THE ENCOUNTER

ALL the while they were talking the new morality
Her eyes explored me.
And when I arose to go
Her fingers were like the tissue
Of a Japanese paper napkin.

TEMPORA

IO! Io! Tamuz!
The Dryad stands in my court-yard
With plaintive, querulous crying.
(Tamuz. Io! Tamuz!)
Oh, no, she is not crying: "Tamuz."
She says, "May my poems be printed this week?
The god Pan is afraid to ask you,
May my poems be printed this week?"

BLACK SLIPPERS: BELLOTTI

AT the table beyond us
With her little suède slippers off,
With her white-stocking'd feet
Carefully kept from the floor by a napkin,
She converses:

> *"Connaissez-vous Ostende?"*

The gurgling Italian lady on the other side of the restaurant
Replies with a certain hauteur,
But I await with patience,
To see how Celestine will re-enter her slippers.
She re-enters them with a groan.

SOCIETY

THE family position was waning,
And on this account the little Aurelia,
Who had laughed on eighteen summers,
Now bears the palsied contact of Phidippus.

IMAGE FROM D'ORLEANS

YOUNG men riding in the street
In the bright new season
Spur without reason,
Causing their steeds to leap.

And at the pace they keep
Their horses' armoured feet
Strike sparks from the cobbled street
In the bright new season.

PAPYRUS

SPRING . . . .
Too long . . . . . .
Gongula . . . . . .

"IONE, DEAD THE LONG YEAR"

EMPTY are the ways,
Empty are the ways of this land
And the flowers
            Bend over with heavy heads.
They bend in vain.
Empty are the ways of this land
                      Where Ione
Walked once, and now does not walk
But seems like a person just gone.

'IMÉPPΩ

THY soul
Grown delicate with satieties,
Atthis.
O Atthis,
I long for thy lips.
I long for thy narrow breasts,
Thou restless, ungathered.

SHOP GIRL

FOR a moment she rested against me
Like a swallow half blown to the wall,
And they talk of Swinburne's women,
And the shepherdess meeting with Guido.
And the harlots of Baudelaire.

TO FORMIANUS' YOUNG LADY FRIEND

AFTER VALERIUS CATULLUS

ALL Hail! young lady with a nose
                by no means too small,
With a foot unbeautiful,
                and with eyes that are not black,
With fingers that are not long, and with a mouth undry,
And with a tongue by no means too elegant,
You are the friend of Formianus, the vendor of cosmetics,
And they call you beautiful in the province,
And you are even compared to Lesbia.

O most unfortunate age!

TAME CAT

"IT rests me to be among beautiful women.
Why should one always lie about such matters?
I repeat:
It rests me to converse with beautiful women
Even though we talk nothing but nonsense,

The purring of the invisible antennæ
Is both stimulating and delightful."

L'ART, 1910

GREEN arsenic smeared on an egg-white cloth,
Crushed strawberries!   Come, let us feast our eyes.

SIMULACRA

WHY does the horse-faced lady of just the unmentionable age
Walk down Longacre reciting Swinburne to herself, inaudibly?
Why does the small child in the soiled-white imitation fur coat

Crawl in the very black gutter beneath the grape stand?
Why does the really handsome young woman approach me in
    Sackville Street
Undeterred by the manifest age of my trappings?

WOMEN BEFORE A SHOP

THE gew-gaws of false amber and false turquoise attract them.
"Like to like nature": these agglutinous yellows!

EPILOGUE

O CHANSONS foregoing
You were a seven days' wonder.
When you came out in the magazines
You created considerable stir in Chicago,
And now you are stale and worn out,
You're a very depleted fashion,
A hoop-skirt, a calash,
An homely, transient antiquity.
Only emotion remains.
Your emotions?
                    Are those of a maître-de-café.

THE SOCIAL ORDER

I

THIS government official
Whose wife is several years his senior,
Has such a caressing air
When he shakes hands with young ladies.

II

(Pompes Funèbres)

This old lady,
Who was "so old that she was an atheist,"
Is now surrounded
By six candles and a crucifix,
While the second wife of a nephew
Makes hay with the things in her house.
Her two cats
Go before her into Avernus;
A sort of chloroformed suttee,
And it is to be hoped that their spirits will walk
With their tails up,
And with a plaintive, gentle mewing,
For it is certain that she has left on this earth
No sound
Save a squabble of female connections.

THE TEA SHOP

THE girl in the tea shop
            Is not so beautiful as she was,
The August has worn against her.
She does not get up the stairs so eagerly;
Yes, she also will turn middle-aged,
And the glow of youth that she spread about us
            As she brought us our muffins
Will be spread about us no longer.
            She also will turn middle-aged.

ANCIENT MUSIC

WINTER is icummen in,
Lhude sing Goddamm,
Raineth drop and staineth slop,
And how the wind doth ramm!
     Sing: Goddamm.
Skiddeth bus and sloppeth us,
An ague hath my ham.
Freezeth river, turneth liver,
     Damn you, sing: Goddamm.
Goddamm, Goddamm, 'tis why I am, Goddamm,
     So 'gainst the winter's balm.
Sing goddamm, damm, sing Goddamm,
Sing goddamm, sing goddamm, DAMM.

NOTE. This is not folk music, but Dr. Ker writes that the tune is to be found under the Latin words of a very ancient canon.

THE LAKE ISLE

O God, O Venus, O Mercury, patron of thieves,
Give me in due time, I beseech you, a little tobacco-shop,
With the little bright boxes
   piled up neatly upon the shelves
And the loose fragrant cavendish
   and the shag,
And the bright Virginia
   loose under the bright glass cases,
And a pair of scales not too greasy,
And the whores dropping in for a word or two in passing,
For a flip word, and to tidy their hair a bit.

O God, O Venus, O Mercury, patron of thieves,
Lend me a little tobacco-shop,
   or install me in any profession
Save this damn'd profession of writing,
   where one needs one's brains all the time.

EPITAPHS

Fu I

FU I loved the high cloud and the hill,
Alas, he died of alcohol.

Li Po

And Li Po also died drunk.
He tried to embrace a moon
In the Yellow River.

OUR CONTEMPORARIES

WHEN the Taihaitian princess
Heard that he had decided,
She rushed out into the sunlight and swarmed up a cocoanut palm
    tree,

But he returned to this island
And wrote ninety Petrarchan sonnets.

NOTE. Il s'agit d'un jeune poète qui a suivi le culte de Gauguin jusqu'à Tahiti même (et qui vit encore). Etant fort bel homme, quand la princesse bistre entendit qu'il voulait lui accorder ses faveurs elle montra son allegresse de la façon dont nous venons de parler. Malheureusement ses poèmes ne sont remplis que de ses propres subjectivités, style Victorien de la "Georgian Anthology."

ANCIENT WISDOM, RATHER COSMIC

CHUANG-TZU dreamed,
And having dreamed that he was a bird, a bee, and a butterfly,
He was uncertain why he should try to feel like anything else,

Hence his contentment.

THE THREE POETS

CANDIDIA has taken a new lover
And three poets are gone into mourning.
The first has written a long elegy to "Chloris,"
To "Chloris chaste and cold," his "only Chloris."
The second has written a sonnet
                              upon the mutability of woman,
And the third writes an epigram to Candidia.

THE GYPSY

*"Est-ce que vous avez vu des autres—des camarades—avec des
singes ou des ours?"*
                          A STRAY GIPSY—A.D. 1912

THAT was the top of the walk, when he said:
"Have you seen any others, any of our lot,
"With apes or bears?"
                          —A brown upstanding fellow
Not like the half-castes,
                          up on the wet road near Clermont.
The wind came, and the rain,
And mist clotted about the trees in the valley,
And I'd the long ways behind me,
                          gray Arles and Biaucaire,
And he said, "Have you seen any of our lot?"
I'd seen a lot of his lot . . .
                          ever since Rhodez,
Coming down from the fair
                          of St. John,
With caravans, but never an ape or a bear.

: 111 :

THE GAME OF CHESS

Dogmatic Statement Concerning the Game of Chess: Theme for a Series of Pictures

RED knights, brown bishops, bright queens,
Striking the board, falling in strong "L's of colour.
Reaching and striking in angles,
                    holding lines in one colour.
This board is alive with light;
                    these pieces are living in form,
Their moves break and reform the pattern:
                    luminous green from the rooks,
Clashing with "X"s of queens,
                    looped with the knight-leaps.

"Y" pawns, cleaving, embanking!
Whirl! Centripetal! Mate! King down in the vortex,
Clash, leaping of bands, straight strips of hard colour,
Blocked lights working in. Escapes. Renewal of contest.

PROVINCIA DESERTA

AT Rochecoart,
Where the hills part
                    in three ways,
And three valleys, full of winding roads,
Fork out to south and north,
There is a place of trees . . . gray with lichen.
I have walked there
                    thinking of old days.
At Chalais
                    is a pleached arbour;
Old pensioners and old protected women
Have the right there—
                    it is charity.

I have crept over old rafters,
                peering down
Over the Dronne,
                over a stream full of lilies.
Eastward the road lies,
                Aubeterre is eastward,
With a garrulous old man at the inn.
I know the roads in that place:
Mareuil to the north-east,
                La Tour,
There are three keeps near Mareuil,
And an old woman,
                glad to hear Arnaut,
Glad to lend one dry clothing.

I have walked
                into Perigord,
I have seen the torch-flames, high-leaping,
Painting the front of that church;
Heard, under the dark, whirling laughter.
I have looked back over the stream
                and seen the high building,
Seen the long minarets, the white shafts.
I have gone in Riberac
                and in Sarlat,
I have climbed rickety stairs, heard talk of Croy,
Walked over En Bertran's old layout,
Have seen Narbonne, and Cahors and Chalus,
Have seen Excideuil, carefully fashioned.

I have said:
                "Here such a one walked.
"Here Cœur-de-Lion was slain.
                "Here was good singing.
"Here one man hastened his step.
                "Here one lay panting."
I have looked south from Hautefort,
                thinking of Montaignac, southward.

I have lain in Rocafixada,
                level with sunset,
Have seen the copper come down
                tingeing the mountains,
I have seen the fields, pale, clear as an emerald,
Sharp peaks, high spurs, distant castles.
I have said: "The old roads have lain here.
"Men have gone by such and such valleys
"Where the great halls were closer together."
I have seen Foix on its rock, seen Toulouse, and
                Arles greatly altered,
I have seen the ruined "Dorata."
                I have said:
"Riquier!   Guido."
                I have thought of the second Troy,
Some little prized place in Auvergnat:
Two men tossing a coin, one keeping a castle,
One set on the highway to sing.
                He sang a woman.
Auvergne rose to the song;
                The Dauphin backed him.
"The castle to Austors!"
                "Pieire kept the singing—
"A fair man and a pleasant."
                He won the lady,
Stole her away for himself, kept her against armed force:
So ends that story.
That age is gone;
Pieire de Maensac is gone.
I have walked over these roads;
I have thought of them living.

CATHAY

FOR THE MOST PART FROM THE CHINESE OF RIHAKU,
FROM THE NOTES OF THE LATE ERNEST
FENOLLOSA, AND THE DECIPHERINGS
OF THE PROFESSORS MORI
AND ARIGA
(1915)

SONG OF THE BOWMEN OF SHU

HERE we are, picking the first fern-shoots
And saying: When shall we get back to our country?
Here we are because we have the Ken-in for our foemen,
We have no comfort because of these Mongols.
We grub the soft fern-shoots,
When anyone says "Return," the others are full of sorrow.
Sorrowful minds, sorrow is strong, we are hungry and thirsty.
Our defence is not yet made sure, no one can let his friend
      return.
We grub the old fern-stalks.
We say: Will we be let to go back in October?
There is no ease in royal affairs, we have no comfort.
Our sorrow is bitter, but we would not return to our country.
What flower has come into blossom?
Whose chariot?   The General's.
Horses, his horses even, are tired.   They were strong.
We have no rest, three battles a month.
By heaven, his horses are tired.
The generals are on them, the soldiers are by them.
The horses are well trained, the generals have ivory arrows and
      quivers ornamented with fish-skin.
The enemy is swift, we must be careful.
When we set out, the willows were drooping with spring,
We come back in the snow,
We go slowly, we are hungry and thirsty,
Our mind is full of sorrow, who will know of our grief?
                                    Bunno (Shih-ching), 167

: 117 :

THE BEAUTIFUL TOILET

BLUE, blue is the grass about the river
And the willows have overfilled the close garden.
And within, the mistress, in the midmost of her youth,
White, white of face, hesitates, passing the door.
Slender, she puts forth a slender hand;

And she was a courtezan in the old days,
And she has married a sot,
Who now goes drunkenly out
And leaves her too much alone.

Attributed to Mei Shêng, 140 B.C.

THE RIVER SONG

THIS boat is of satō-wood, and its gunwales are cut magnolia,
Musicians with jewelled flutes and with pipes of gold
Fill full the sides in rows, and our wine
Is rich for a thousand cups.
We carry singing girls, drift with the drifting water,
Yet Sennin needs
A yellow stork for a charger, and all our seamen
Would follow the white gulls or ride them.
Kutsu's prose song
Hangs with the sun and moon.

King So's terraced palace
       is now but barren hill,
But I draw pen on this barge
Causing the five peaks to tremble,
And I have joy in these words
       like the joy of blue islands.
(If glory could last forever
Then the waters of Han would flow northward.)

* * *

And I have moped in the Emperor's garden, awaiting an
    order-to-write!
I looked at the dragon-pond, with its willow-coloured water
Just reflecting the sky's tinge,
And heard the five-score nightingales aimlessly singing.

The eastern wind brings the green colour into the island grasses at
    Ei-shū,
The purple house and the crimson are full of Spring softness.
South of the pond the willow-tips are half-blue and bluer,
Their cords tangle in mist, against the brocade-like palace.
Vine-strings a hundred feet long hang down from carved railings,
And high over the willows, the fine birds sing to each other, and
    listen,
Crying—"Ken-kwan" for the early wind, and the feel of it.
The wind bundles itself into a bluish cloud and wanders off.
Over a thousand gates, over a thousand doors are the sounds of
    spring singing,
And the Emperor is at Kō.
Five clouds hang aloft, bright on the purple sky,
The imperial guards come forth from the golden house with their
    armour a-gleaming.
The Emperor in his jewelled car goes out to inspect his flowers,
He goes out to Hōrai, to look at the wing-flapping storks,
He returns by way of Shi rock, to hear the new nightingales,
For the gardens at Jō-rin are full of new nightingales,
Their sound is mixed in this flute,
Their voice is in the twelve pipes here.

By Rihaku (Li T'ai Po), 8th century A.D.

THE RIVER-MERCHANT'S WIFE:
A LETTER

WHILE my hair was still cut straight across my forehead
I played about the front gate, pulling flowers.
You came by on bamboo stilts, playing horse,
You walked about my seat, playing with blue plums.
And we went on living in the village of Chōkan:
Two small people, without dislike or suspicion.

At fourteen I married My Lord you.
I never laughed, being bashful.
Lowering my head, I looked at the wall.
Called to, a thousand times, I never looked back.

At fifteen I stopped scowling,
I desired my dust to be mingled with yours
Forever and forever and forever.
Why should I climb the look out?

At sixteen you departed,
You went into far Ku-tō-en, by the river of swirling eddies,
And you have been gone five months.
The monkeys make sorrowful noise overhead.

You dragged your feet when you went out.
By the gate now, the moss is grown, the different mosses,
Too deep to clear them away!
The leaves fall early this autumn, in wind.
The paired butterflies are already yellow with August
Over the grass in the West garden;
They hurt me.   I grow older.
If you are coming down through the narrows of the river Kiang,
Please let me know beforehand,
And I will come out to meet you
          As far as Chō-fū-Sa.

By Rihaku (Li T'ai Po)

POEM BY THE BRIDGE AT TEN-SHIN

MARCH has come to the bridge head,
Peach boughs and apricot boughs hang over a thousand gates,
At morning there are flowers to cut the heart,
And evening drives them on the eastward-flowing waters.
Petals are on the gone waters and on the going,
   And on the back-swirling eddies,
But to-day's men are not the men of the old days,
Though they hang in the same way over the bridge-rail.

The sea's colour moves at the dawn
And the princes still stand in rows, about the throne,
And the moon falls over the portals of Sei-jō-yō,
And clings to the walls and the gate-top.
With head gear glittering against the cloud and sun,
The lords go forth from the court, and into far borders.
They ride upon dragon-like horses,
Upon horses with head-trappings of yellow metal,
And the streets make way for their passage.
   Haughty their passing,
Haughty their steps as they go in to great banquets,
To high halls and curious food,
To the perfumed air and girls dancing,
To clear flutes and clear singing;
To the dance of the seventy couples;
To the mad chase through the gardens.
Night and day are given over to pleasure
And they think it will last a thousand autumns,
   Unwearying autumns.
For them the yellow dogs howl portents in vain,
And what are they compared to the lady Ryokushu,
   That was cause of hate!
Who among them is a man like Han-rei
   Who departed alone with his mistress,
With her hair unbound, and he his own skiffsman!
      By Rihaku (Li T'ai Po)

THE JEWEL STAIRS' GRIEVANCE

THE jewelled steps are already quite white with dew,
It is so late that the dew soaks my gauze stockings,
And I let down the crystal curtain
And watch the moon through the clear autumn.

By Rihaku (Li T'ai Po)

NOTE. Jewel stairs, therefore a palace. Grievance, therefore there is something to complain of. Gauze stockings, therefore a court lady, not a servant who complains. Clear autumn, therefore she has no excuse on account of weather. Also she has come early, for the dew has not merely whitened the stairs, but has soaked her stockings. The poem is especially prized because she utters no direct reproach.

LAMENT OF THE FRONTIER GUARD

BY the North Gate, the wind blows full of sand,
Lonely from the beginning of time until now!
Trees fall, the grass goes yellow with autumn.
I climb the towers and towers
      to watch out the barbarous land:
Desolate castle, the sky, the wide desert.
There is no wall left to this village.
Bones white with a thousand frosts,
High heaps, covered with trees and grass;
Who brought this to pass?
Who has brought the flaming imperial anger?
Who has brought the army with drums and with kettle-drums?
Barbarous kings.
A gracious spring, turned to blood-ravenous autumn,
A turmoil of wars-men, spread over the middle kingdom,
Three hundred and sixty thousand,
And sorrow, sorrow like rain.
Sorrow to go, and sorrow, sorrow returning.
Desolate, desolate fields,

And no children of warfare upon them,
No longer the men for offence and defence.
Ah, how shall you know the dreary sorrow at the North Gate,
With Riboku's name forgotten,
And we guardsmen fed to the tigers.

By Rihaku (Li T'ai Po)

EXILE'S LETTER

TŌ So-Kiu of Rakuyō, ancient friend, Chancellor Gen.
Now I remember that you built me a special tavern
By the south side of the bridge at Ten-shin.
With yellow gold and white jewels, we paid for songs and laughter
And we were drunk for month on month, forgetting the kings and
    princes.
Intelligent men came drifting in from the sea and from the west
    border,
And with them, and with you especially
There was nothing at cross purpose,
And they made nothing of sea-crossing or of mountain-crossing,
If only they could be of that fellowship,
And we all spoke out our hearts and minds, and without regret.
And then I was sent off to South Wai,
    smothered in laurel groves,
And you to the north of Raku-hoku,
Till we had nothing but thoughts and memories in common.
And then, when separation had come to its worst,
We met, and travelled into Sen-jō,
Through all the thirty-six folds of the turning and twisting waters,
Into a valley of the thousand bright flowers,
That was the first valley;
And into ten thousand valleys full of voices and pine-winds.
And with silver harness and reins of gold,
Out came the East of Kan foreman and his company.
And there came also the "True man" of Shi-yō to meet me,

Playing on a jewelled mouth-organ.
In the storied houses of San-ka they gave us more Sennin music,
Many instruments, like the sound of young phœnix broods.
The foreman of Kan-chū, drunk, danced
       because his long sleeves wouldn't keep still
With that music playing,
And I, wrapped in brocade, went to sleep with my head on his lap,
And my spirit so high it was all over the heavens,
And before the end of the day we were scattered like stars, or rain.
I had to be off to So, far away over the waters,
You back to your river-bridge.

And your father, who was brave as a leopard,
Was governor in Hei Shu, and put down the barbarian rabble.
And one May he had you send for me,
          despite the long distance.
And what with broken wheels and so on, I won't say it wasn't hard
       going,
Over roads twisted like sheep's guts.
And I was still going, late in the year,
          in the cutting wind from the North,
And thinking how little you cared for the cost,
          and you caring enough to pay it.
And what a reception:
Red jade cups, food well set on a blue jewelled table,
And I was drunk, and had no thought of returning.
And you would walk out with me to the western corner of the
       castle,
To the dynastic temple, with water about it clear as blue jade,
With boats floating, and the sound of mouth-organs and drums,
With ripples like dragon-scales, going grass green on the water,
Pleasure lasting, with courtezans, going and coming without
       hindrance,
With the willow flakes falling like snow,
And the vermilioned girls getting drunk about sunset,
And the water, a hundred feet deep, reflecting green eyebrows
—Eyebrows painted green are a fine sight in young moonlight,
Gracefully painted—

And the girls singing back at each other,
Dancing in transparent brocade,
And the wind lifting the song, and interrupting it,
Tossing it up under the clouds.
      And all this comes to an end.
      And is not again to be met with.
I went up to the court for examination,
Tried Yō Yū's luck, offered the Chōyō song,
And got no promotion,
      and went back to the East Mountains
      White-headed.
And once again, later, we met at the South bridge-head.
And then the crowd broke up, you went north to San palace,
And if you ask how I regret that parting:
It is like the flowers falling at Spring's end
      Confused, whirled in a tangle.
What is the use of talking, and there is no end of talking,
There is no end of things in the heart.
I call in the boy,
Have him sit on his knees here
      To seal this,
And send it a thousand miles, thinking.

By Rihaku (Li T'ai Po)

FOUR POEMS OF DEPARTURE

Light rain is on the light dust
The willows of the inn-yard
Will be going greener and greener,
But you, Sir, had better take wine ere your departure,
For you will have no friends about you
When you come to the gates of Yō.

(ŌMAKITSU [Wang Wei])

SEPARATION ON THE RIVER KIANG

KO-JIN goes west from Kō-kaku-ro,
The smoke-flowers are blurred over the river.
His lone sail blots the far sky.
And now I see only the river,
    The long Kiang, reaching heaven.

Rihaku (Li T'ai Po)

TAKING LEAVE OF A FRIEND

BLUE mountains to the north of the walls,
White river winding about them;
Here we must make separation
And go out through a thousand miles of dead grass.

Mind like a floating wide cloud,
Sunset like the parting of old acquaintances
Who bow over their clasped hands at a distance.
Our horses neigh to each other
    as we are departing.

Rihaku (Li T'ai Po)

LEAVE-TAKING NEAR SHOKU

"Sansō, King of Shoku, built roads"

THEY say the roads of Sansō are steep,
Sheer as the mountains.
The walls rise in a man's face,
Clouds grow out of the hill
     at his horse's bridle.
Sweet trees are on the paved way of the Shin,
Their trunks burst through the paving,
And freshets are bursting their ice
     in the midst of Shoku, a proud city.

Men's fates are already set,
There is no need of asking diviners.

               Rihaku (Li T'ai Po)

THE CITY OF CHŌAN

THE phœnix are at play on their terrace.
The phœnix are gone, the river flows on alone.
Flowers and grass
Cover over the dark path
     where lay the dynastic house of the Go.
The bright cloths and bright caps of Shin
Are now the base of old hills.

The Three Mountains fall through the far heaven,
The isle of White Heron
     splits the two streams apart.
Now the high clouds cover the sun
And I can not see Chōan afar
And I am sad.

               Rihaku (Li T'ai Po)

SOUTH-FOLK IN COLD COUNTRY

THE Dai horse neighs against the bleak wind of Etsu,
The birds of Etsu have no love for En, in the north,
Emotion is born out of habit.
Yesterday we went out of the Wild-Goose gate,
To-day from the Dragon-Pen.*
Surprised. Desert turmoil. Sea sun.
Flying snow bewilders the barbarian heaven.
Lice swarm like ants over our accoutrements.
Mind and spirit drive on the feathery banners.
Hard fight gets no reward.
Loyalty is hard to explain.
Who will be sorry for General Rishōgun,
            the swift moving,
Whose white head is lost for this province?
                    Rihaku (*Li T'ai Po*)

---

* *I.e.*, we have been warring from one end of the empire to the other, now east, now west, on each border.

SENNIN POEM BY KAKUHAKU (KUO P'U)

THE red and green kingfishers
            flash between the orchids and clover,
One bird casts its gleam on another.

Green vines hang through the high forest,
They weave a whole roof to the mountain,
The lone man sits with shut speech,
He purrs and pats the clear strings.
He throws his heart up through the sky,
He bites through the flower pistil
            and brings up a fine fountain.
The red-pine-tree god looks at him and wonders.
He rides through the purple smoke to visit the sennin,

He takes "Floating Hill"* by the sleeve,
He claps his hand on the back of the great water sennin.

But you, you dam'd crowd of gnats,
Can you even tell the age of a turtle?

* Name of a sennin.

A BALLAD OF THE MULBERRY ROAD

THE sun rises in south east corner of things
To look on the tall house of the Shin
For they have a daughter named Rafu, (pretty girl)
She made the name for herself: "Gauze Veil,"
For she feeds mulberries to silkworms.
She gets them by the south wall of the town.
With green strings she makes the warp of her basket,
She makes the shoulder-straps of her basket
          from the boughs of Katsura,
And she piles her hair up on the left side of her head-piece.

Her earrings are made of pearl,
Her underskirt is of green pattern-silk,
Her overskirt is the same silk dyed in purple,
And when men going by look on Rafu
          They set down their burdens,
They stand and twirl their moustaches.
          Anonymous (Fenollosa MSS., very early; Mori's gloze)

OLD IDEA OF CHŌAN BY ROSHŌRIN
(LU CHAO-LIN)

I

THE narrow streets cut into the wide highway at Chōan,
Dark oxen, white horses,
   drag on the seven coaches with outriders.
The coaches are perfumed wood,
The jewelled chair is held up at the crossway,
Before the royal lodge:
A glitter of golden saddles, awaiting the princess;
They eddy before the gate of the barons.
The canopy embroidered with dragons
   drinks in and casts back the sun.
Evening comes.
   The trappings are bordered with mist.
The hundred cords of mist are spread through
   and double the trees,
Night birds, and night women,
Spread out their sounds through the gardens.

II

Birds with flowery wing, hovering butterflies
   crowd over the thousand gates,
Trees that glitter like jade,
   terraces tinged with silver,
The seed of a myriad hues,
A net-work of arbours and passages and covered ways,
Double towers, winged roofs,
   border the net-work of ways:
A place of felicitous meeting.
Riŏ's house stands out on the sky,
   with glitter of colour
As Butei of Kan had made the high golden lotus
   to gather his dews,
Before it another house which I do not know:
How shall we know all the friends
   whom we meet on strange roadways?

TO-EM-MEI'S "THE UNMOVING CLOUD"

"Wet springtime," says To-em-mei,
"Wet spring in the garden."

I

THE clouds have gathered, and gathered,
       and the rain falls and falls,
The eight ply of the heavens
       are all folded into one darkness,
And the wide, flat road stretches out.
I stop in my room toward the East, quiet, quiet,
I pat my new cask of wine.
My friends are estranged, or far distant,
I bow my head and stand still.

II

Rain, rain, and the clouds have gathered,
The eight ply of the heavens are darkness,
The flat land is turned into river.
       "Wine, wine, here is wine!"
I drink by my eastern window.
I think of talking and man,
And no boat, no carriage, approaches.

III

The trees in my east-looking garden
       are bursting out with new twigs,
They try to stir new affection,

And men say the sun and moon keep on moving
       because they can't find a soft seat.

IV

The birds flutter to rest in my tree,
       and I think I have heard them saying,
"It is not that there are no other men
But we like this fellow the best,
But however we long to speak
He can not know of our sorrow."
       T'ao Yüan-ming (T'ao Ch'ien), A.D. 365–427

POEMS FROM
BLAST
(1914)

SALUTATION THE THIRD

LET us deride the smugness of "The Times":   GUFFAW!
      So much for the gagged reviewers,
It will pay them when the worms are wriggling in their vitals;
These are they who objected to newness,
Here are their tomb-stones.
      They supported the gag and the ring:
A little BLACK BOX contains them.
      So shall you be also,
You slut-bellied obstructionist,
You sworn foe to free speech and good letters,
You fungus, you continuous gangrene.

Come, let us on with the new deal,
      Let us be done with pandars and jobbery,
Let us spit upon those who pat the big-bellies for profit,
Let us go out in the air a bit.

Or perhaps I *will* die at thirty?
Perhaps you will have the pleasure of defiling my pauper's grave;
I wish you joy, I proffer you all my assistance.
It has been your habit for long
      to do away with good writers,
You either drive them mad, or else you blink at their suicides,
Or else you condone their drugs,
      and talk of insanity and genius,
But I will not go mad to please you,
      I will not flatter you with an early death,
Oh, no, I will stick it out,
      Feel your hates wriggling about my feet
As a pleasant tickle,
      to be observed with derision,
Though many move with suspicion,
      Afraid to say that they hate you;
The taste of my boot?
      Here is the taste of my boot,
Caress it,
      lick off the blacking.

MONUMENTUM AERE, ETC.

YOU say that I take a good deal upon myself;
That I strut in the robes of assumption.

In a few years no one will remember the *buffo*,
No one will remember the trivial parts of me,
The comic detail will be absent.
As for you, you will rot in the earth,
And it is doubtful if even your manure will be rich enough

To keep grass
Over your grave.

COME MY CANTILATIONS

COME my cantilations,
Let us dump our hatreds into one bunch and
be done with them,
Hot sun, clear water, fresh wind,
Let me be free of pavements,
Let me be free of the printers.
Let come beautiful people
Wearing raw silk of good colour,
Let come the graceful speakers,
Let come the ready of wit,
Let come the gay of manner, the insolent and the exulting.
We speak of burnished lakes,
Of dry air, as clear as metal.

BEFORE SLEEP

1

THE lateral vibrations caress me,
They leap and caress me,
They work pathetically in my favour,
They seek my financial good.

She of the spear stands present.
The gods of the underworld attend me, O Annubis,
These are they of thy company.
With a pathetic solicitude they attend me;
Undulant,
Their realm is the lateral courses.

2
Light!

I am up to follow thee, Pallas.
Up and out of their caresses.
You were gone up as a rocket,
Bending your passages from right to left and from
      left to right
In the flat projection of a spiral.
The gods of drugged sleep attend me,
Wishing me well;
I am up to follow thee, Pallas.

POST MORTEM CONSPECTU

A BROWN, fat babe sitting in the lotus,
And you were glad and laughing
With a laughter not of this world.
It is good to splash in the water
And laughter is the end of all things.

FRATRES MINORES

WITH minds still hovering above their testicles
Certain poets here and in France
Still sigh over established and natural fact
Long since fully discussed by Ovid.
They howl.   They complain in delicate and exhausted metres
That the twitching of three abdominal nerves
Is incapable of producing a lasting Nirvana.

POEMS FROM
LUSTRA
(1915)

NEAR PERIGORD

A Perigord, pres del muralh
Tan que i puosch' om gitar ab malh.

YOU'D have men's hearts up from the dust
And tell their secrets, Messire Cino,
Right enough?   Then read between the lines of Uc St. Circ,
Solve me the riddle, for you know the tale.

Bertrans, En Bertrans, left a fine canzone:
"Maent, I love you, you have turned me out.
The voice at Montfort, Lady Agnes' hair,
Bel Miral's stature, the viscountess' throat,
Set all together, are not worthy of you. . . ."
And all the while you sing out that canzone,
Think you that Maent lived at Montagnac,
One at Chalais, another at Malemort
Hard over Brive—for every lady a castle,
Each place strong.

       Oh, *is* it easy enough?
Tairiran held hall in Montagnac,
His brother-in-law was all there was of power
In Perigord, and this good union
Gobbled all the land, and held it later for some hundred years.
And our En Bertrans was in Altafort,
Hub of the wheel, the stirrer-up of strife,
As caught by Dante in the last wallow of hell—
The headless trunk "that made its head a lamp,"
For separation wrought out separation,
And he who set the strife between brother and brother
And had his way with the old English king,
Viced in such torture for the "counterpass."

How would you live, with neighbours set about you—
Poictiers and Brive, untaken Rochecouart,
Spread like the finger-tips of one frail hand;
And you on that great mountain of a palm—
Not a neat ledge, not Foix between its streams,

But one huge back half-covered up with pine,
Worked for and snatched from the string-purse of Born—
The four round towers, four brothers—mostly fools:
What could he do but play the desperate chess,
And stir old grudges?
   "Pawn your castles, lords!
Let the Jews pay."
   And the great scene—
(That, maybe, never happened!)
   Beaten at last,
Before the hard old king:
   "Your son, ah, since he died
"My wit and worth are cobwebs brushed aside
"In the full flare of grief. Do what you will."

 Take the whole man, and ravel out the story.
He loved this lady in castle Montagnac?
The castle flanked him—he had need of it.
You read to-day, how long the overlords of Perigord,
The Talleyrands, have held the place; it was no transient fiction.
And Maent failed him? Or saw through the scheme?

 And all his net-like thought of new alliance?
Chalais is high, a-level with the poplars.
Its lowest stones just meet the valley tips
Where the low Dronne is filled with water-lilies.
And Rochecouart can match it, stronger yet,
The very spur's end, built on sheerest cliff,
And Malemort keeps its close hold on Brive,
While Born, his own close purse, his rabbit warren,
His subterranean chamber with a dozen doors,
A-bristle with antennæ to feel roads,
To sniff the traffic into Perigord.
And that hard phalanx, that unbroken line,
The ten good miles from there to Maent's castle,
All of his flank—how could he do without her?
And all the road to Cahors, to Toulouse?
What would he do without her?

"Papiol,
Go forthright singing—Anhes, Cembelins.
There is a throat; ah, there are two white hands;
There is a trellis full of early roses,
And all my heart is bound about with love.
Where am I come with compound flatteries—
What doors are open to fine compliment?"
And every one half jealous of Maent?
He wrote the catch to pit their jealousies
Against her; give her pride in them?

Take his own speech, make what you will of it—
And still the knot, the first knot, of Maent?

    Is it a love poem?   Did he sing of war?
Is it an intrigue to run subtly out,
Born of a jongleur's tongue, freely to pass
Up and about and in and out the land,
Mark him a craftsman and a strategist?
(St. Leider had done as much as Polhonac,
Singing a different stave, as closely hidden.)
Oh, there is precedent, legal tradition,
To sing one thing when your song means another,
"*Et albirar ab lor bordon*—"
Foix' count knew that.   What is Sir Bertrans' singing?
Maent, Maent, and yet again Maent,
Or war and broken heaumes and politics?

II

    End fact.   Try fiction.   Let us say we see
En Bertrans, a tower-room at Hautefort,
Sunset, the ribbon-like road lies, in red cross-light,
Southward toward Montagnac, and he bends at a table
Scribbling, swearing between his teeth; by his left hand
Lie little strips of parchment covered over,
Scratched and erased with *al* and *ochaisos*.
Testing his list of rhymes, a lean man?   Bilious?
With a red straggling beard?
And the green cat's-eye lifts toward Montagnac.

Or take his "magnet" singer setting out,
Dodging his way past Aubeterre, singing at Chalais
      In the vaulted hall,
Or, by a lichened tree at Rochecouart
Aimlessly watching a hawk above the valleys,
Waiting his turn in the mid-summer evening,
Thinking of Aelis, whom he loved heart and soul . . .
To find her half alone, Montfort away,
And a brown, placid, hated woman visiting her,
Spoiling his visit, with a year before the next one.
Little enough?
Or carry him forward. "Go through all the courts,
My Magnet," Bertrans had said.

      We came to Ventadour
In the mid love court, he sings out the canzon,
No one hears save Arrimon Luc D'Esparo—
No one hears aught save the gracious sound of compliments.
Sir Arrimon counts on his fingers, Montfort,
Rochecouart, Chalais, the rest, the tactic,
Malemort, guesses beneath, sends word to Cœur-de-Lion:
The compact, de Born smoked out, trees felled
About his castle, cattle driven out!
Or no one sees it, and En Bertrans prospered?

      And ten years after, or twenty, as you will,
Arnaut and Richard lodge beneath Chalus:
The dull round towers encroaching on the field,
The tents tight drawn, horses at tether
Further and out of reach, the purple night,
The crackling of small fires, the bannerets,
The lazy leopards on the largest banner,
Stray gleams on hanging mail, an armourer's torch-flare
Melting on steel.

      And in the quietest space
They probe old scandals, say de Born is dead;
And we've the gossip (skipped six hundred years).
Richard shall die to-morrow—leave him there

Talking of *trobar clus* with Daniel.
And the "best craftsman" sings out his friend's song,
Envies its vigour . . . and deplores the technique,
Dispraises his own skill?—That's as you will.
And they discuss the dead man,
Plantagenet puts the riddle: "Did he love her?"
And Arnaut parries: "Did he love your sister?
True, he has praised her, but in some opinion
He wrote that praise only to show he had
The favour of your party; had been well received."

"You knew the man."
          "*You* knew the man."
"I am an artist, you have tried both métiers."
"You were born near him."
          "Do we know our friends?"
"Say that he saw the castles, say that he loved Maent!"
"Say that he loved her, does it solve the riddle?"
  End the discussion, Richard goes out next day
And gets a quarrel-bolt shot through his vizard,
Pardons the bowman, dies,

          Ends our discussion.   Arnaut ends
"In sacred odour"—(that's apocryphal!)
And we can leave the talk till Dante writes:
Surely I saw, and still before my eyes
Goes on that headless trunk, that bears for light
Its own head swinging, gripped by the dead hair,
And like a swinging lamp that says, "Ah me!
I severed men, my head and heart
Ye see here severed, my life's counterpart."

Or take En Bertrans?

III

Ed eran due in uno, ed uno in due;
Inferno, XXVIII, 125

BEWILDERING spring, and by the Auvezere
Poppies and day's eyes in the green émail
Rose over us; and we knew all that stream,
And our two horses had traced out the valleys;
Knew the low flooded lands squared out with poplars,
In the young days when the deep sky befriended.
      And great wings beat above us in the twilight,
And the great wheels in heaven
Bore us together . . . surging . . . and apart . . .
Believing we should meet with lips and hands,

  High, high and sure . . . and then the counterthrust:
'Why do you love me? Will you always love me?
But I am like the grass, I can not love you.'
Or, 'Love, and I love and love you,
And hate your mind, not *you*, your soul, your hands.'

      So to this last estrangement, Tairiran!

      There shut up in his castle, Tairiran's,
She who had nor ears nor tongue save in her hands,
Gone—ah, gone—untouched, unreachable!
She who could never live save through one person,
She who could never speak save to one person,
And all the rest of her a shifting change,
A broken bundle of mirrors . . . !

VILLANELLE: THE PSYCHOLOGICAL HOUR

I HAD over-prepared the event,
        that much was ominous.
With middle-ageing care
        I had laid out just the right books.
I had almost turned down the pages.

        Beauty is so rare a thing.
        So few drink of my fountain.

So much barren regret,
So many hours wasted!
And now I watch, from the window,
        the rain, the wandering busses.

"Their little cosmos is shaken"—
        the air is alive with that fact.
In their parts of the city
        they are played on by diverse forces.
How do I know?
        Oh, I know well enough.
For them there is something afoot.
        As for me;
I had over-prepared the event—

        Beauty is so rare a thing
        So few drink of my fountain.

Two friends: a breath of the forest . . .
Friends? Are people less friends
    because one has just, at last, found them?
Twice they promised to come.

        "Between the night and morning?"

Beauty would drink of my mind.
Youth would awhile forget
        my youth is gone from me.

II

("Speak up!   You have danced so stiffly?
    Someone admired your works,
    And said so frankly.

    "Did you talk like a fool,
    The first night?
    The second evening?"

"*But* they promised again:
      'To-morrow at tea-time.'")

III

Now the third day is here—
      no word from either;
No word from her nor him,
Only another man's note:
      "Dear Pound, I am leaving England."

DANS UN OMNIBUS DE LONDRES

LES yeux d'une morte
M'ont salué,
Enchassés dans un visage stupide
Dont tous les autres traits étaient banals,
Ils m'ont salué
Et alors je vis bien des choses
Au dedans de ma mémoire
Remuer,
S'éveiller.

Je vis des canards sur le bord d'un lac minuscule,
Auprès d'un petit enfant gai, bossu.

Je vis les colonnes anciennes en "toc"
Du Parc Monceau,
Et deux petites filles graciles,

Des patriciennes,
        aux toisons couleur de lin,
Et des pigeonnes
Grasses
        comme des poulardes.
Je vis le parc,
Et tous les gazons divers
Où nous avions loué des chaises
Pour quatre sous.

Je vis les cygnes noirs,
Japonais,
Leurs ailes
Teintées de couleur sang-de-dragon,
Et toutes les fleurs
D'Armenonville.

Les yeux d'une morte
M'ont salué.

PAGANI'S, NOVEMBER 8

SUDDENLY discovering in the eyes of the very beautiful
        Normande cocotte
The eyes of the very learned British Museum assistant.

TO A FRIEND WRITING
ON CABARET DANCERS

"Breathe not the word to-morrow in her ears"
Vir Quidem, on Dancers

GOOD "Hedgethorn," for we'll anglicize your name
Until the last slut's hanged and the last pig disemboweled,
Seeing your wife is charming and your child
Sings in the open meadow—at least the kodak says so—

My good fellow, you, on a cabaret silence
And the dancers, you write a sonnet;

Say "Forget To-morrow," being of all men
The most prudent, orderly, and decorous!

"Pepita" has no to-morrow, so you write.

Pepita has such to-morrows: with the hands puffed out,
The pug-dog's features encrusted with tallow
Sunk in a frowsy collar—an unbrushed black.
She will not bathe too often, but her jewels
Will be a stuffy, opulent sort of fungus
Spread on both hands and on the up-pushed-bosom—
It juts like a shelf between the jowl and corset.

Have you, or I, seen most of cabarets, good Hedgethorn?

Here's Pepita, tall and slim as an Egyptian mummy,
Marsh-cranberries, the ribbed and angular pods
Flare up with scarlet orange on stiff stalks
And so Pepita
Flares on the crowded stage before our tables
Or slithers about between the dishonest waiters—

> "Carmen est maigre, un trait de bistre
> Cerne son œil de gitana"

And "rend la flamme,"
    you know the deathless verses.

: 150 :

I search the features, the avaricious features
Pulled by the kohl and rouge out of resemblance —
Six pence the object for a change of passion.

"Write me a poem."
            Come now, my dear Pepita,
"-ita, bonita, chiquita,"
That's what you mean you advertising spade,
Or take the intaglio, my fat great-uncle's heirloom:
Cupid, astride a phallus with two wings,
Swinging a cat-o'-nine-tails.
            No.   Pepita,
I have seen through the crust.
            I don't know what you look like
But your smile pulls one way
            and your painted grin another,
While that cropped fool,
            that tom-boy who can't earn her living,
Come, come to-morrow,
            To-morrow in ten years at the latest,
She will be drunk in the ditch, but you, Pepita,
Will be quite rich, quite plump, with pug-bitch features,
With a black tint staining your cuticle,
Prudent and svelte Pepita.
            "Poète, writ me a poème!"
Spanish and Paris, love of the arts part of your
            geisha-culture!

Euhenia, in short skirts, slaps her wide stomach,
Pulls up a roll of fat for the pianist,
"Pauvre femme maigre!" she says.
            He sucks his chop bone,
That some one else has paid for,
            grins up an amiable grin,
Explains the decorations.
            Good Hedgethorn, they all have futures,
All these people.
            Old Popkoff

Will dine next week with Mrs. Basil,
Will meet a duchess and an ex-diplomat's widow
From Weehawken—who has never known
Any but "Majesties" and Italian nobles.
Euhenia will have a *fonda* in Orbajosa.
The amorous nerves will give way to digestive;
"Delight thy soul in fatness," saith the preacher.
We can't preserve the elusive *"mica salis,"*
It may last well in these dark northern climates,
Nell Gwynn's still here, despite the reformation,
And Edward's mistresses still light the stage,
A glamour of classic youth in their deportment.
The prudent whore is not without her future,
Her bourgeois dulness is deferred.

> Her present dulness . . .
Oh well, her present dulness . . .

Now in Venice, 'Storante al Giardino, I went early,
Saw the performers come: him, her, the baby,
A quiet and respectable-tawdry trio;
An hour later: a show of calves and spangles,

"Un e duo fanno tre,"
> Night after night,
No change, no change of program, *"Che!*
"La donna è mobile."

HOMAGE TO QUINTUS SEPTIMIUS FLORENS CHRISTIANUS

(Ex libris Graecæ)

I

THEODORUS will be pleased at my death,
And someone else will be pleased at the death of Theodorus,
And yet everyone speaks evil of death.

II

This place is the Cyprian's for she has ever the fancy
To be looking out across the bright sea,
Therefore the sailors are cheered, and the waves
Keep small with reverence, beholding her image.

Anyte

III

A sad and great evil is the expectation of death—
And there are also the inane expenses of the funeral;
Let us therefore cease from pitying the dead
For after death there comes no other calamity.

Palladas

IV

Troy

Whither, O city, are your profits and your gilded shrines,
And your barbecues of great oxen,
And the tall women walking your streets, in gilt clothes,
With their perfumes in little alabaster boxes?
Where is the work of your home-born sculptors?

Time's tooth is into the lot, and war's and fate's too.
Envy has taken your all,
Save your douth and your story.

Agathias Scholasticus

V

Woman?   Oh, woman is a consummate rage,
          but dead, or asleep, she pleases.
Take her.   She has two excellent seasons.

Palladas

VI

Nicarchus upon Phidon his doctor

Phidon neither purged me, nor touched me,
But I remembered the name of his fever medicine
                              and died.

FISH AND THE SHADOW

THE salmon-trout drifts in the stream,
The soul of the salmon-trout floats over the stream
                    Like a little wafer of light.

The salmon moves in the sun-shot, bright shallow sea. . . .

As light as the shadow of the fish
                    that falls through the water,
She came into the large room by the stair,
Yawning a little she came with the sleep still upon her.

"I am just from bed.   The sleep is still in my eyes.
"Come.   I have had a long dream."
And I: "That wood?
"And two springs have passed us."
"Not so far, no, not so far now,
There is a place—but no one else knows it—
A field in a valley . . .
                              Qu'ieu sui avinen,
Ieu lo sai."

She must speak of the time
Of Arnaut de Mareuil, I thought, *"qu'ieu sui avinen."*

Light as the shadow of the fish
That falls through the pale green water.

: 154 :

IMPRESSIONS OF FRANÇOIS-MARIE AROUET (DE VOLTAIRE)

I

Phyllidula and the Spoils of Gouvernet

WHERE, Lady, are the days
When you could go out in a hired hansom
Without footmen and equipments?
And dine in a soggy, cheap restaurant?
Phyllidula now, with your powdered Swiss footman
Clanking the door shut,
      and lying;
And carpets from Savonnier, and from Persia,
And your new service at dinner,
And plates from Germain,
And cabinets and chests from Martin (almost lacquer),
And your white vases from Japan,
And the lustre of diamonds,
Etcetera, etcetera, and etcetera?

II

To Madame du Châtelet

If you'd have me go on loving you
Give me back the time of the thing.

Will you give me dawn light at evening?
Time has driven me out from the fine plaisaunces,
The parks with the swards all over dew,
And grass going glassy with the light on it,
The green stretches where love is and the grapes
Hang in yellow-white and dark clusters ready for pressing.

And if now we can't fit with our time of life
There is not much but its evil left us.

Life gives us two minutes, two seasons—
      One to be dull in;
Two deaths—and to stop loving and being lovable,

That is the real death,
The other is little beside it.

Crying after the follies gone by me,
Quiet talking is all that is left us—
Gentle talking, not like the first talking, less lively;
And to follow after friendship, as they call it,
Weeping that we can follow naught else.

III

To Madame Lullin

You'll wonder that an old man of eighty
Can go on writing you verses. . . .

Grass showing under the snow,
Birds singing late in the year!

And Tibullus could say of his death, in his Latin:
"Delia, I would look on you, dying."

And Delia herself fading out,
Forgetting even her beauty.

END OF LUSTRA

PHANOPOEIA

I

ROSE WHITE, YELLOW, SILVER

THE swirl of light follows me through the square,
The smoke of incense
Mounts from the four horns of my bed-posts,
The water-jet of gold light bears us up through the ceilings;
Lapped in the gold-coloured flame I descend through the æther.
The silver ball forms in my hand,
It falls and rolls to your feet.

II

SALTUS

The swirling sphere has opened
     and you are caught up to the skies,
You are englobed in my sapphire.
                   Io! Io!

You have perceived the blades of the flame
The flutter of sharp-edged sandals.

The folding and lapping brightness
Has held in the air before you.
You have perceived the leaves of the flame.

III

CONCAVA VALLIS

The wire-like bands of colour involute mount from my fingers;
I have wrapped the wind round your shoulders
And the molten metal of your shoulders
     bends into the turn of the wind,

AOI!
The whirling tissue of light
     is woven and grows solid beneath us;
The sea-clear sapphire of air, the sea-dark clarity,
     stretches both sea-cliff and ocean.

LANGUE D'OC

Alba

WHEN *the nightingale to his mate*
Sings day-long and night late
My love and I keep state
In bower,
In flower,
'Till the watchman on the tower
Cry:

      "Up! *Thou rascal, Rise,*
    I see the white
        Light
          And the night
            Flies."

I

Compleynt of a gentleman who has been waiting
outside for some time

O PLASMATOUR and true celestial light,
Lord powerful, engirdlèd all with might,
Give my good-fellow aid in fools' despite
Who stirs not forth this night,
                    And day comes on.
"Sst! my good fellow, art awake or sleeping?
Sleep thou no more. I see the star upleaping
That hath the dawn in keeping,
                    And day comes on!
"Hi! Harry, hear me, for I sing aright
Sleep not thou now, I hear the bird in flight
That plaineth of the going of the night,
                    And day comes on!
"Come now! Old swenkin! Rise up from thy bed,
I see the signs upon the welkin spread,
If thou come not, the cost be on thy head.
                    And day comes on!
"And here I am since going down of sun,

And pray to God that is St. Mary's son,
To bring thee safe back, my companion.
                                And day comes on.
"And thou out here beneath the porch of stone
Badest me to see that a good watch was done,
And now thou'lt none of me, and wilt have none
                                Of song of mine."
            (*Bass voice from inside.*)
"Wait, my good fellow.   For such joy I take
With her venust and noblest to my make
To hold embracèd, and will not her forsake
For yammer of the cuckold,
                                Though day break."
                                (*Girart Bornello.*)

II

Avril

WHEN the springtime is sweet
And the birds repeat
Their new song in the leaves,
'Tis meet
A man go where he will.

But from where my heart is set
No message I get;
My heart all wakes and grieves;
Defeat
Or luck, I must have my fill.

Our love comes out
Like the branch that turns about
On the top of the hawthorne,
With frost and hail at night
Suffers despite
'Till the sun come, and the green leaf on the bough.

I remember the young day
When we set strife away,

And she gave me such gesning,
Her love and her ring:
God grant I die not by any man's stroke
'Till I have my hand 'neath her cloak.

I care not for their clamour
Who have come between me and my charmer,
For I know how words run loose,
Big talk and little use.
Spoilers of pleasure,
We take their measure.

(*Guilhem de Peitieu.*)

III

Descant on a Theme by Cerclamon
WHEN the sweet air goes bitter,
And the cold birds twitter
Where the leaf falls from the twig,
I sough and sing

       that Love goes out
       Leaving me no power to hold him.

Of love I have naught
Save trouble and sad thought,
And nothing is grievous
       as I desirous,
Wanting only what
No man can get or has got.

With the noblest that stands in men's sight,
If all the world be in despite
       I care not a glove.
Where my love is, there is a glitter of sun;
God give me life, and let my course run

       'Till I have her I love
       To lie with and prove.

I do not live, nor cure me,
Nor feel my ache—great as it is,
For love will give
      me no respite,
Nor do I know when I turn left or right
      nor when I go out.

        For in her is all my delight
        And all that can save me.

I shake and burn and quiver
From love, awake and in swevyn,
Such fear I have she deliver
              me not from pain,
      Who know not how to ask her;
      Who can not.
Two years, three years I seek
And though I fear to speak out,
      Still she must know it.

If she won't have me now, Death is my portion,
      Would I had died that day
      I came into her sway.
God! How softly this kills!
When her love look steals on me.
Killed me she has, I know not how it was,
      For I would not look on a woman.

Joy I have none, if she make me not mad
      Or set me quiet, or bid me chatter.
Good is it to me if she flout
      Or turn me inside out, and about.
      My ill doth she turn sweet.

How swift it is.
      For I am traist and loose,
      I am true, or a liar,
      All vile, or all gentle,
      Or shaking between,
              as she desire,

I, Cerclamon, sorry and glad,
        The man whom love had
                        and has ever;
        Alas! who'er it please or pain,
        She can me retain.

I am gone from one joy,
From one I loved never so much,
        She by one touch
        Reft me away;
        So doth bewilder me
        I can not say my say
                        nor my desire,
        And when she looks on me
        It seems to me
                        I lose all wit and sense.

        The noblest girls men love
        'Gainst her I prize not as a glove
        Worn and old.
        Though the whole world run rack
        And go dark with cloud,
        Light is
        Where she stands,
        And a clamour loud
                        in my ears.

IV

Vergier

IN orchard under the hawthorne
She has her lover till morn,
Till the traist man cry out to warn
Them. God how swift the night,
                        And day comes on.

O Plasmatour, that thou end not the night,
Nor take my belovèd from my sight,

Nor I, nor tower-man, look on daylight,
'Fore God, How swift the night,
                        And day comes on.

"Lovely thou art, to hold me close and kisst,
  Now cry the birds out, in the meadow mist,
  Despite the cuckold, do thou as thou list,
  So swiftly goes the night
                        And day comes on.

"My pretty boy, make we our play again
  Here in the orchard where the birds complain,
  'Till the traist watcher his song unrein,
  Ah God!   How swift the night
                        And day comes on."

"Out of the wind that blows from her,
  That dancing and gentle is and thereby pleasanter,
  Have I drunk a draught, sweeter than scent of myrrh.
  Ah God!   How swift the night.
                        And day comes on."

Venust the lady, and none lovelier,
For her great beauty, many men look on her,
Out of my love will her heart not stir.
By God, how swift the night.
                        And day comes on.

MŒURS CONTEMPORAINES

I

Mr. Styrax   1

MR. HECATOMB STYRAX, the owner of a large estate
       and of large muscles,
A "blue" and a climber of mountains, has married
       at the age of 28,
He being at that age a virgin,
The term "virgo" being made male in mediaeval latinity;
       His ineptitudes
Have driven his wife from one religious excess to
       another.
She has abandoned the vicar
For he was lacking in vehemence;
She is now the high-priestess
Of a modern and ethical cult,
          And even now Mr. Styrax
          Does not believe in aesthetics.

2

His brother has taken to gipsies,
But the son-in-law of Mr. H. Styrax
Objects to perfumed cigarettes.
          In the parlance of Niccolo Machiavelli:
          "Thus things proceed in their circle";
          And thus the empire is maintained.

II

Clara

AT sixteen she was a potential celebrity
With a distaste for caresses.
She now writes to me from a convent;
Her life is obscure and troubled;
Her second husband will not divorce her;
Her mind is, as ever, uncultivated,
And no issue presents itself.
She does not desire her children,

Or any more children.
Her ambition is vague and indefinite,
She will neither stay in, nor come out.

III

Soirée
UPON learning that the mother wrote verses,
And that the father wrote verses,
And that the youngest son was in a publisher's office,
And that the friend of the second daughter was
       undergoing a novel,
The young American pilgrim
Exclaimed:
      "This is a darn'd clever bunch!"

IV

Sketch 48 b. II
AT the age of 27
Its home mail is still opened by its maternal parent
And its office mail may be opened by
      its parent of the opposite gender.
It is an officer,
      and a gentleman,
            and an architect.

V

"Nodier raconte . . ."   1
AT a friend of my wife's there is a photograph,
A faded, pale brownish photograph,
Of the times when the sleeves were large,
Silk, stiff and large above the *lacertus*,
That is, the upper arm,
And décolleté. . . .
      It is a lady,
She sits at a harp,
Playing,

And by her left foot, in a basket,
Is an infant, aged about 14 months,
The infant beams at the parent,
The parent re-beams at its offspring.
The basket is lined with satin,
There is a satin-like bow on the harp.

2

And in the home of the novelist
There is a satin-like bow on an harp.
You enter and pass hall after hall,
Conservatory follows conservatory,
Lilies lift their white symbolical cups,
Whence their symbolical pollen has been excerpted,
Near them I noticed an harp
And the blue satin ribbon,
And the copy of "Hatha Yoga"
And the neat piles of unopened, unopening books,

And she spoke to me of the monarch,
And of the purity of her soul.

VI

Stele

AFTER years of continence
    he hurled himself into a sea of six women.
Now, quenched as the brand of Meleagar,
    he lies by the poluphloisboious sea-coast.

Παρὰ θῖνα πολυφλοίο βοιο θαλάσσης.

SISTE VIATOR.

VII

I Vecchii

THEY will come no more,
The old men with beautiful manners.

Il était comme un tout petit garçon
With his blouse full of apples
And sticking out all the way round;
Blagueur!   "Con gli occhi onesti e tardi,"

And he said:
        "Oh!   Abelard!"   as if the topic
Were much too abstruse for his comprehension,
And he talked about "the Great Mary,"
And said: "Mr. Pound is shocked at my levity."
When it turned out he meant Mrs. Ward.

And the other was rather like my bust by Gaudier,
Or like a real Texas colonel,
He said: "Why flay dead horses?
"There was once a man called Voltaire."

And he said they used to cheer Verdi,
In Rome, after the opera,
And the guards couldn't stop them,

And that was an anagram for Vittorio
Emanuele Re D' Italia,
And the guards couldn't stop them.

        Old men with beautiful manners,
Sitting in the Row of a morning;
Walking on the Chelsea Embankment.

VIII

Ritratto

AND she said:

       "You remember Mr. Lowell,
"He was your ambassador here?"
And I said: "That was before I arrived."
And she said:

       "He stomped into my bedroom. . . .
(By that time she had got on to Browning.)
". . . stomped into my bedroom. . . .
"And said: 'Do I,
"'I ask you, Do I
"'Care too much for society dinners?'
"And I wouldn't say that he didn't.
"Shelley used to live in this house."

She was a very old lady,
I never saw her again.

CANTICO DEL SOLE

FROM "INSTIGATIONS"

THE thought of what America would be like
If the Classics had a wide circulation
    Troubles my sleep,
The thought of what America,
The thought of what America,
The thought of what America would be like
If the Classics had a wide circulation
    Troubles my sleep.
Nunc dimittis, now lettest thou thy servant,
Now lettest thou thy servant
    Depart in peace.
The thought of what America,
The thought of what America,
The thought of what America would be like
If the Classics had a wide circulation . . .
    Oh well!
    It troubles my sleep.

NOTE FOR "CANTICO DEL SOLE"

This poem formed the conclusion of Pound's essay "The Classics 'Escape'," printed originally in the *Little Review* for March 1918 and collected in *Instigations* (1920). (The poem as printed in *Instigations* is followed by the Latin "*Oravimus*" [we have prayed]). In that essay Pound had printed Section 211 of the United States Criminal Code—on obscene publications—and quoted a recent decision from "a learned judge" that some

> *approved publications at times escape [the law] only because they come within the term "classics," which means, for the purpose of the application of the statute, that they are ordinarily immune from interference, because they have the sanction of age and fame and* USUALLY APPEAL TO A COMPARATIVELY LIMITED NUMBER OF READERS [Pound's capitals].

The idea that "Our literature . . . is subject to the taste of one individual . . . selected without any examination of his literary qualifications" outraged Pound; but he considered the matter far too serious to be written of in anger. Instead he expressed his feelings in the cadences of the "Cantico del Sole" of St. Francis of Assisi. For Pound's version of the Italian original see *The Spirit of Romance* (1910), pp. 88–89.

—DONALD GALLUP

Hugh Selwyn Mauberley

(LIFE AND CONTACTS)

The sequence is so distinctly a farewell to London that the reader
who chooses to regard this as an exclusively American edition
may as well omit it and turn at once to page 189.

"VOCAT ÆSTUS IN UMBRAM"
Nemesianus, Ec. IV.

E. P. ODE POUR L'ELECTION
DE SON SEPULCHRE

I

FOR three years, out of key with his time,
He strove to resuscitate the dead art
Of poetry; to maintain "the sublime"
In the old sense.   Wrong from the start—

No, hardly, but seeing he had been born
In a half savage country, out of date;
Bent resolutely on wringing lilies from the acorn;
Capaneus; trout for factitious bait;

Ἴδμεν γάρ τοι πάνθ᾽, ὅσ᾽ ἐνὶ Τροίῃ
Caught in the unstopped ear;
Giving the rocks small lee-way
The chopped seas held him, therefore, that year.

His true Penelope was Flaubert,
He fished by obstinate isles;
Observed the elegance of Circe's hair
Rather than the mottoes on sun-dials.

Unaffected by "the march of events,"
He passed from men's memory in *l'an trentuniesme*
De son eage; the case presents
No adjunct to the Muses' diadem.

II

THE age demanded an image
Of its accelerated grimace,
Something for the modern stage,
Not, at any rate, an Attic grace;

Not, not certainly, the obscure reveries
Of the inward gaze;
Better mendacities
Than the classics in paraphrase!

The "age demanded" chiefly a mould in plaster,
Made with no loss of time,
A prose kinema, not, not assuredly, alabaster
Or the "sculpture" of rhyme.

III

THE tea-rose tea-gown, etc.
Supplants the mousseline of Cos,
The pianola "replaces"
Sappho's barbitos.

Christ follows Dionysus,
Phallic and ambrosial
Made way for macerations;
Caliban casts out Ariel.

All things are a flowing,
Sage Heracleitus says;
But a tawdry cheapness
Shall outlast our days.

Even the Christian beauty
Defects—after Samothrace;
We see τὸ καλόν
Decreed in the market place.

Faun's flesh is not to us,
Nor the saint's vision.
We have the press for wafer;
Franchise for circumcision.

All men, in law, are equals.
Free of Pisistratus,
We choose a knave or an eunuch
To rule over us.

O bright Apollo,
τίν' ἄνδρα, τίν' ἥρωα, τινα θεόν,

What god, man, or hero
Shall I place a tin wreath upon!

IV

THESE fought in any case,
and some believing,
                pro domo, in any case . . .

Some quick to arm,
some for adventure,
some from fear of weakness,
some from fear of censure,
some for love of slaughter, in imagination,
learning later . . .
some in fear, learning love of slaughter;

Died some, pro patria,
                non "dulce" non "et decor" . . .
walked eye-deep in hell
believing in old men's lies, then unbelieving
come home, home to a lie,
home to many deceits,
home to old lies and new infamy;
usury age-old and age-thick
and liars in public places.

Daring as never before, wastage as never before.
Young blood and high blood,
fair cheeks, and fine bodies;

fortitude as never before

frankness as never before,
disillusions as never told in the old days,
hysterias, trench confessions,
laughter out of dead bellies.

V

THERE died a myriad,
And of the best, among them,
For an old bitch gone in the teeth,
For a botched civilization,

Charm, smiling at the good mouth,
Quick eyes gone under earth's lid,

For two gross of broken statues,
For a few thousand battered books.

YEUX GLAUQUES

GLADSTONE was still respected,
When John Ruskin produced
"Kings' Treasuries"; Swinburne
And Rossetti still abused.

Fœtid Buchanan lifted up his voice
When that faun's head of hers
Became a pastime for
Painters and adulterers.

The Burne-Jones cartons
Have preserved her eyes;
Still, at the Tate, they teach
Cophetua to rhapsodize;

Thin like brook-water,
With a vacant gaze.
The English Rubaiyat was still-born
In those days.

The thin, clear gaze, the same
Still darts out faun-like from the half-ruin'd face,
Questing and passive. . . .
"Ah, poor Jenny's case" . . .

Bewildered that a world
Shows no surprise
At her last maquero's
Adulteries.

"SIENA MI FE'; DISFECEMI MAREMMA"

AMONG the pickled fœtuses and bottled bones,
Engaged in perfecting the catalogue,
I found the last scion of the
Senatorial families of Strasbourg, Monsieur Verog.

For two hours he talked of Galliffet;
Of Dowson; of the Rhymers' Club;
Told me how Johnson (Lionel) died
By falling from a high stool in a pub . . .

But showed no trace of alcohol
At the autopsy, privately performed—
Tissue preserved—the pure mind
Arose toward Newman as the whiskey warmed.

Dowson found harlots cheaper than hotels;
Headlam for uplift; Image impartially imbued
With raptures for Bacchus, Terpsichore and the Church.
So spoke the author of "The Dorian Mood,"

M. Verog, out of step with the decade,
Detached from his contemporaries,
Neglected by the young,
Because of these reveries.

BRENNBAUM

THE sky-like limpid eyes,
The circular infant's face,
The stiffness from spats to collar
Never relaxing into grace;

The heavy memories of Horeb, Sinai and the forty years,
Showed only when the daylight fell
Level across the face
Of Brennbaum "The Impeccable."

MR. NIXON

IN the cream gilded cabin of his steam yacht
Mr. Nixon advised me kindly, to advance with fewer
Dangers of delay.   "Consider
        "Carefully the reviewer.

"I was as poor as you are;
"When I began I got, of course,
"Advance on royalties, fifty at first," said Mr. Nixon,
"Follow me, and take a column,
"Even if you have to work free.

"Butter reviewers. From fifty to three hundred
"I rose in eighteen months;
"The hardest nut I had to crack
"Was Dr. Dundas.

"I never mentioned a man but with the view
"Of selling my own works.
"The tip's a good one, as for literature
"It gives no man a sinecure.

"And no one knows, at sight, a masterpiece.
"And give up verse, my boy,
"There's nothing in it."

. . . .

Likewise a friend of Blougram's once advised me:
Don't kick against the pricks,
Accept opinion. The "Nineties" tried your game
And died, there's nothing in it.

X

BENEATH the sagging roof
The stylist has taken shelter,
Unpaid, uncelebrated,
At last from the world's welter

Nature receives him;
With a placid and uneducated mistress
He exercises his talents
And the soil meets his distress.

The haven from sophistications and contentions
Leaks through its thatch;
He offers succulent cooking;
The door has a creaking latch.

XI

"CONSERVATRIX of Milésien"
Habits of mind and feeling,
Possibly. But in Ealing
With the most bank-clerkly of Englishmen?

No, "Milésian" is an exaggeration.
No instinct has survived in her
Older than those her grandmother
Told her would fit her station.

XII

"DAPHNE with her thighs in bark
Stretches toward me her leafy hands,"—
Subjectively.   In the stuffed-satin drawing-room
I await The Lady Valentine's commands,

Knowing my coat has never been
Of precisely the fashion
To stimulate, in her,
A durable passion;

Doubtful, somewhat, of the value
Of well-gowned approbation
Of literary effort,
But never of The Lady Valentine's vocation:

Poetry, her border of ideas,
The edge, uncertain, but a means of blending
With other strata
Where the lower and higher have ending;

A hook to catch the Lady Jane's attention,
A modulation toward the theatre,
Also, in the case of revolution,
A possible friend and comforter.
.   .   .   .

Conduct, on the other hand, the soul
"Which the highest cultures have nourished"
To Fleet St. where
Dr. Johnson flourished;

Beside this thoroughfare
The sale of half-hose has
Long since superseded the cultivation
Of Pierian roses.

ENVOI (1919)

GO, *dumb-born book,*
Tell her that sang me once that song of Lawes:
Hadst thou but song
As thou hast subjects known,
Then were there cause in thee that should condone
Even my faults that heavy upon me lie,
And build her glories their longevity.

Tell her that sheds
Such treasure in the air,
Recking naught else but that her graces give
Life to the moment,
I would bid them live
As roses might, in magic amber laid,
Red overwrought with orange and all made
One substance and one colour
Braving time.

Tell her that goes
With song upon her lips
But sings not out the song, nor knows
The maker of it, some other mouth,
May be as fair as hers,
Might, in new ages, gain her worshippers,
When our two dusts with Waller's shall be laid,
Siftings on siftings in oblivion,
Till change hath broken down
All things save Beauty alone.

MAUBERLEY (1920)

"Vacuos exercet in aera morsus."

I

TURNED from the "eau-forte
Par Jacquemart"
To the strait head
Of Messalina:

"His true Penelope
Was Flaubert,"
And his tool
The engraver's.

Firmness,
Not the full smile,
His art, but an art
In profile;

Colourless
Pier Francesca,
Pisanello lacking the skill
To forge Achaia.

II

"Qu'est ce qu'ils savent de l'amour, et qu'est ce qu'ils peuvent en comprendre?

"S'ils ne comprennent pas la poésie, s'ils ne sentent pas la musique, qu'est ce qu'ils peuvent comprendre de cette passion en comparaison avec laquelle la rose est grossière et le parfum des violettes un tonnerre?"   CAID ALI

FOR three years, diabolus in the scale,
He drank ambrosia,
All passes, ANANGKE prevails,
Came end, at last, to that Arcadia.

He had moved amid her phantasmagoria,
Amid her galaxies,
NUKTIS 'AGALMA
·   ·   ·   ·   ·   ·   ·

Drifted . . . drifted precipitate,
Asking time to be rid of . . .
Of his bewilderment; to designate
His new found orchid. . . .

To be certain . . . certain . . .
(Amid ærial flowers) . . . time for arrangements—
Drifted on
To the final estrangement;

Unable in the supervening blankness
To sift TO AGATHON from the chaff
Until he found his sieve . . .
Ultimately, his seismograph:

—Given that is his "fundamental passion,"
This urge to convey the relation
Of eye-lid and cheek-bone
By verbal manifestation;

To present the series
Of curious heads in medallion—

He had passed, inconscient, full gaze,
The wide-banded irides
And botticellian sprays implied
In their diastasis;

Which anæthesis, noted a year late,
And weighed, revealed his great affect,
(Orchid), mandate
Of Eros, a retrospect.

   . . .

Mouths biting empty air,
The still stone dogs,
Caught in metamorphosis, were
Left him as epilogues.

"THE AGE DEMANDED"

Vide Poem II. Page 173

FOR this agility chance found
Him of all men, unfit
As the red-beaked steeds of
The Cytheræan for a chain bit.

The glow of porcelain
Brought no reforming sense
To his perception
Of the social inconsequence.

Thus, if her colour
Came against his gaze,
Tempered as if
It were through a perfect glaze

He made no immediate application
Of this to relation of the state
To the individual, the month was more temperate
Because this beauty had been.

The coral isle, the lion-coloured sand
Burst in upon the porcelain revery:
Impetuous troubling
Of his imagery.

Mildness, amid the neo-Nietzschean clatter,
His sense of graduations,
Quite out of place amid
Resistance to current exacerbations,

Invitation, mere invitation to perceptivity
Gradually led him to the isolation
Which these presents place
Under a more tolerant, perhaps, examination.

By constant elimination
The manifest universe
Yielded an armour
Against utter consternation,

A Minoan undulation,
Seen, we admit, amid ambrosial circumstances
Strengthened him against
The discouraging doctrine of chances,

And his desire for survival,
Faint in the most strenuous moods,
Became an Olympian *apathein*
In the presence of selected perceptions.

A pale gold, in the aforesaid pattern,
The unexpected palms
Destroying, certainly, the artist's urge,
Left him delighted with the imaginary
Audition of the phantasmal sea-surge,

Incapable of the least utterance or composition,
Emendation, conservation of the "better tradition,"
Refinement of medium, elimination of superfluities,
August attraction or concentration.

Nothing, in brief, but maudlin confession,
Irresponse to human aggression,
Amid the precipitation, down-float
Of insubstantial manna,
Lifting the faint susurrus
Of his subjective hosannah.

Ultimate affronts to
Human redundancies;

Non-esteem of self-styled "his betters"
Leading, as he well knew,
To his final
Exclusion from the world of letters.

IV

SCATTERED Moluccas
Not knowing, day to day,
The first day's end, in the next noon;
The placid water
Unbroken by the Simoon;

Thick foliage
Placid beneath warm suns,
Tawn fore-shores
Washed in the cobalt of oblivions;

Or through dawn-mist
The grey and rose
Of the juridical
Flamingoes;

A consciousness disjunct,
Being but this overblotted
Series
Of intermittences;

Coracle of Pacific voyages,
The unforecasted beach;
Then on an oar
Read this:

"I was
"And I no more exist;
"Here drifted
"An hedonist."

MEDALLION

LUINI in porcelain!
The grand piano
Utters a profane
Protest with her clear soprano.

The sleek head emerges
From the gold-yellow frock
As Anadyomene in the opening
Pages of Reinach.

Honey-red, closing the face-oval,
A basket-work of braids which seem as if they were
Spun in King Minos' hall
From metal, or intractable amber;

The face-oval beneath the glaze,
Bright in its suave bounding-line, as,
Beneath half-watt rays,
The eyes turn topaz.

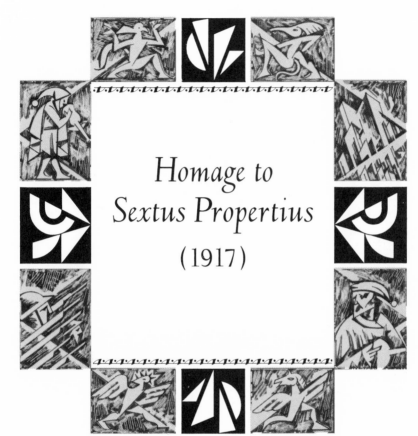

Homage to
Sextus Propertius

(1917)

Orfeo

"Quia pauper amavi."

I

SHADES of Callimachus, Coan ghosts of Philetas
It is in your grove I would walk,
I who come first from the clear font
Bringing the Grecian orgies into Italy,
                              and the dance into Italy.
Who hath taught you so subtle a measure,
                              in what hall have you heard it;
What foot beat out your time-bar,
                     what water has mellowed your whistles?

Out-weariers of Apollo will, as we know, continue their Martian
     generalities,
     We have kept our erasers in order.
A new-fangled chariot follows the flower-hung horses;
A young Muse with young loves clustered about her
                     ascends with me into the æther, . . .
And there is no high-road to the Muses.

Annalists will continue to record Roman reputations,
Celebrities from the Trans-Caucasus will belaud Roman celebrities
And expound the distentions of Empire,
But for something to read in normal circumstances?
For a few pages brought down from the forked hill unsullied?
I ask a wreath which will not crush my head.
                              And there is no hurry about it;
I shall have, doubtless, a boom after my funeral,
Seeing that long standing increases all things
                              regardless of quality.

And who would have known the towers
                     pulled down by a deal-wood horse;
Or of Achilles withstaying waters by Simois
Or of Hector spattering wheel-rims,
Or of Polydmantus, by Scamander, or Helenus and Deiphoibos?
Their door-yards would scarcely know them, or Paris.
Small talk O Ilion, and O Troad
                     twice taken by Oetian gods,
If Homer had not stated your case!

And I also among the later nephews of this city

                           shall have my dog's day,

With no stone upon my contemptible sepulchre;

My vote coming from the temple of Phoebus in Lycia, at Patara,

And in the mean time my songs will travel,

And the devirginated young ladies will enjoy them

                    when they have got over the strangeness,

For Orpheus tamed the wild beasts—

                  and held up the Threician river;

And Citharaon shook up the rocks by Thebes

           and danced them into a bulwark at his pleasure,

And you, O Polyphemus?   Did harsh Galatea almost

Turn to your dripping horses, because of a tune, under Aetna?

We must look into the matter.

Bacchus and Apollo in favour of it,

There will be a crowd of young women doing homage to my
    palaver,

Though my house is not propped up by Taenarian columns from
    Laconia (associated with Neptune and Cerberus),

Though it is not stretched upon gilded beams;

My orchards do not lie level and wide

                 as the forests of Phaecia,

                 the luxurious and Ionian,

Nor are my caverns stuffed stiff with a Marcian vintage,

My cellar does not date from Numa Pompilius,

Nor bristle with wine jars,

Nor is it equipped with a frigidaire patent;

Yet the companions of the Muses

              will keep their collective nose in my books,

And weary with historical data, they will turn to my dance tune.

Happy who are mentioned in my pamphlets,

    the songs shall be a fine tomb-stone over their beauty.

      But against this?

Neither expensive pyramids scraping the stars in their route,

Nor houses modelled upon that of Jove in East Elis,

Nor the monumental effigies of Mausolus,

            are a complete elucidation of death.

Flame burns, rain sinks into the cracks
And they all go to rack ruin beneath the thud of the years.
Stands genius a deathless adornment,
                    a name not to be worn out with the years.

II

I HAD been seen in the shade, recumbent on cushioned Helicon,
The water dripping from Bellerophon's horse,
Alba, your kings, and the realm your folk
                    have constructed with such industry
Shall be yawned out on my lyre—with such industry.
My little mouth shall gobble in such great fountains,
"Wherefrom father Ennius, sitting before I came, hath drunk."

I had rehearsed the Curian brothers, and made remarks on the
        Horatian javelin
(Near Q. H. Flaccus' book-stall).
"Of" royal Aemilia, drawn on the memorial raft,
"Of" the victorious delay of Fabius, and the left-
                    handed battle at Cannae,
Of lares fleeing the "Roman seat" . . .
                    I had sung of all these
And of Hannibal,
                    and of Jove protected by geese.
And Phoebus looking upon me from the Castalian tree,
Said then "You idiot! What are you doing with that water:
"Who has ordered a book about heroes?
                    "You need, Propertius, not think
"About acquiring that sort of a reputation.
        "Soft fields must be worn by small wheels,
"You pamphlets will be thrown, thrown often into a chair
"Where a girl waits alone for her lover;
        "Why wrench your page out of its course?
"No keel will sink with your genius
        "Let another oar churn the water,
"Another wheel, the arena; mid-crowd is as bad as mid-sea."
He had spoken, and pointed me a place with his plectrum:

Orgies of vintages, an earthern image of Silenus
Strengthened with rushes, Tegaean Pan,
The small birds of the Cytharean mother,
                    their Punic faces dyed in the Gorgon's lake;
Nine girls, from as many countrysides
                    bearing her offerings in their unhardened hands,

Such my cohort and setting.   And she bound ivy to his thyrsos;
Fitted song to the strings;
                                        Roses twined in her hands.
And one among them looked at me with face offended,
Calliope:
        "Content ever to move with white swans!
"Nor will the noise of high horses lead you ever to battle;
"Nor will the public criers ever have your name
                                        in their classic horns,
"Nor Mars shout you in the wood at Aeonium,
                        Nor where Rome ruins German riches,
"Nor where the Rhine flows with barbarous blood,
                        and flood carries wounded Suevi.
"Obviously crowned lovers at unknown doors,
"Night dogs, the marks of a drunken scurry,
"These are your images, and from you the sorcer-
                                izing of shut-in young ladies,
"The wounding of austere men by chicane."
        Thus Mistress Calliope,
        Dabbling her hands in the fount, thus she
Stiffened our face with the backwash of Philetas the Coan.

III

MIDNIGHT, and a letter comes to me from
            our mistress:
        Telling me to come to Tibur:

                                                        At once!!
"Bright tips reach up from twin towers,
"Anienan spring water falls into flat-spread pools."

What *is* to be done about it?
    Shall I entrust myself to entangled shadows,
Where bold hands may do violence to my person?

Yet if I postpone my obedience
                        because of this respectable terror,
I shall be prey to lamentations worse than a nocturnal assailant.
And I shall be in the wrong,
                        and it will last a twelve month,
For her hands have no kindness me-ward,

Nor is there anyone to whom lovers are not sacred at midnight
    And in the Via Sciro.
If any man would be a lover
                        he may walk on the Scythian coast,
No barbarism would go to the extent of doing him harm,
The moon will carry his candle,
                        the stars will point out the stumbles,
Cupid will carry lighted torches before him
                        and keep mad dogs off his ankles.
Thus all roads are perfectly safe
                        and at any hour;
Who so indecorous as to shed the pure gore of a suitor?!
    Cypris is his cicerone.

What if undertakers follow my track,
                        such a death is worth dying.
She would bring frankincense and wreaths to my tomb,
    She would sit like an ornament on my pyre.

God's aid, let not my bones lie in a public location
With crowds too assiduous in their crossing of it;
For thus are tombs of lovers most desecrated.

May a woody and sequestered place cover me with its foliage
Or may I inter beneath the hummock
                        of some as yet uncatalogued sand;
At any rate I shall not have my epitaph in a high road.

IV

TELL me the truths which you hear of our constant young lady,
   Lygdamus,
And may the bought yoke of a mistress lie with
    equitable weight on your shoulders;
For I am swelled up with inane pleasurabilities
    and deceived by your reference
To things which you think I would like to believe.

No messenger should come wholly empty,
    and a slave should fear plausibilities;
Much conversation is as good as having a home.
  Out with it, tell it to me, all of it, from the beginning,
I guzzle with outstretched ears.
Thus? She wept into uncombed hair,

          And you saw it.
Vast waters flowed from her eyes?

        You, you Lygdamus
Saw her stretched on her bed, —

       it was no glimpse in a mirror;
No gawds on her snowy hands, no orfevrerie,
Sad garment draped on her slender arms.
Her escritoires lay shut by the bed-feet.
Sadness hung over the house, and the desolated female attendants
Were desolated because she had told them her dreams.

She was veiled in the midst of that place,
Damp woolly handkerchiefs were stuffed into her undryable eyes,
And a querulous noise responded to our solicitous reprobations.
For which things you will get a reward from me,
   Lygdamus?
To say many things is equal to having a home.
And the other woman "has not enticed me
      by her pretty manners,
"She has caught me with herbaceous poison,
     she twiddles the spiked wheel of a rhombus,

"She stews puffed frogs, snake's bones, the moulted feathers of
    screech owls,

"She binds me with ravvles of shrouds.
            "Black spiders spin in her bed!
"Let her lovers snore at her in the morning!
            "May the gout cramp up her feet!
"Does he like me to sleep here alone,
            Lygdamus?
"Will he say nasty things at my funeral?"

And you expect me to believe this
                        after twelve months of discomfort?

                        V
                        1
NOW if ever it is time to cleanse Helicon;
            to lead Emathian horses afield,
And to name over the census of my chiefs in the Roman camp.
If I have not the faculty, "The bare attempt would be
    praise-worthy."
"In things of similar magnitude
                the mere will to act is sufficient."

The primitive ages sang Venus,
                        the last sings of a tumult,
And I also will sing war when this matter of a girl is exhausted.
I with my beak hauled ashore would proceed in a more stately
    manner,
My Muse is eager to instruct me in a new gamut, or gambetto,
Up, up my soul, from your lowly cantilation,
                        put on a timely vigour.

Oh august Pierides! Now for a large-mouthed product.
Thus:
"The Euphrates denies its protection to the Parthian and
    apologizes for Crassus,"

And "It is, I think, India which now gives necks to your triumph,"
And so forth, Augustus. "Virgin Arabia shakes in her inmost
    dwelling."
If any land shrink into a distant seacoast,
                    it is a mere postponement of your domination.
And I shall follow the camp, I shall be duly celebrated for singing
    the affairs of your cavalry.
May the fates watch over my day.

2

Yet you ask on what account I write so many love-lyrics
And whence this soft book comes into my mouth.
Neither Calliope nor Apollo sung these things into my ear,
    My genius is no more than a girl.

If she with ivory fingers drive a tune through the lyre,
    We look at the process.
How easy the moving fingers; if hair is mussed on her forehead,
If she goes in a gleam of Cos, in a slighter of dyed stuff,
There is a volume in the matter; if her eyelids sink into sleep,
There are new jobs for the author;
And if she plays with me with her shirt off,
    We shall construct many Iliads.
And whatever she does or says
    We shall spin long yarns out of nothing.

Thus much the fates have allotted me, and if, Maecenas,
I were able to lead heroes into armour, I would not,
Neither would I warble of Titans, nor of Ossa
                    spiked onto Olympus,
Nor of causeways over Pelion,
Nor of Thebes in its ancient respectability,
                  nor of Homer's reputation in Pergamus,
Nor of Xerxes' two-barreled kingdom, nor of Remus and his royal
    family,
Nor of dignified Carthaginian characters,
Nor of Welsh mines and the profit Marus had out of them.

I should remember Caesar's affairs . . .

                                         for a background,
Although Callimachus did without them,

                                 and without Theseus,
Without an inferno, without Achilles attended of gods,
Without Ixion, and without the sons of Menoetius and the Argo
    and without Jove's grave and the Titans.

And my ventricles do not palpitate to Caesarial *ore rotundos*,
Nor to the tune of the Phrygian fathers.
Sailor, of winds; a plowman, concerning his oxen;
Soldier, the enumeration of wounds; the sheep-feeder, of ewes;
We, in our narrow bed, turning aside from battles:
Each man where he can, wearing out the day in his manner.

3

It is noble to die of love, and honourable to remain
                                 uncuckolded for a season.
And she speaks ill of light women,

                         and will not praise Homer
Because Helen's conduct is "unsuitable."

VI

WHEN, when, and whenever death closes our eyelids,
Moving naked over Acheron
Upon the one raft, victor and conquered together,
Marius and Jugurtha together,

                              one tangle of shadows.

Caesar plots against India,
Tigris and Euphrates shall, from now on, flow at his bidding,
Tibet shall be full of Roman policemen,
The Parthians shall get used to our statuary

                       and acquire a Roman religion;
One raft on the veiled flood of Acheron,
    Marius and Jugurtha together.

Nor at my funeral either will there be any long trail,
                                   bearing ancestral lares and images;
No trumpets filled with my emptiness,
Nor shall it be on an Atalic bed;
             The perfumed cloths shall be absent.
A small plebeian procession.
             Enough, enough and in plenty
There will be three books at my obsequies
Which I take, my not unworthy gift, to Persephone.

You will follow the bare scarified breast
Nor will you be weary of calling my name, nor too weary
             To place the last kiss on my lips
When the Syrian onyx is broken.

                         "He who is now vacant dust
                         "Was once the slave of one passion:"
Give that much inscription

                         "Death why tardily come?"

You, sometimes, will lament a lost friend,
             For it is a custom:
This care for past men,

Since Adonis was gored in Idalia, and the Cytharean
Ran crying with out-spread hair,
             In vain, you call back the shade,
In vain, Cynthia.   Vain call to unanswering shadow,
             Small talk comes from small bones.

                         VII

ME happy, night, night full of brightness;
Oh couch made happy by my long delectations;
How many words talked out with abundant candles;
Struggles when the lights were taken away;
Now with bared breasts she wrestled against me,
             Tunic spread in delay;

And she then opening my eyelids fallen in sleep,
Her lips upon them; and it was her mouth saying:
     Sluggard!

In how many varied embraces, our changing arms,
Her kisses, how many, lingering on my lips.
"Turn not Venus into a blinded motion,
        Eyes are the guides of love,
Paris took Helen naked coming from the bed of Menelaus,
Endymion's naked body, bright bait for Diana,"
        —such at least is the story.

While our fates twine together, sate we our eyes with love;
For long night comes upon you
                        and a day when no day returns.
Let the gods lay chains upon us
                    so that no day shall unbind them.

Fool who would set a term to love's madness,
For the sun shall drive with black horses,
        earth shall bring wheat from barley,
The flood shall move toward the fountain
        Ere love know moderations,
        The fish shall swim in dry streams.
No, now while it may be, let not the fruit of life cease.

                    Dry wreaths drop their petals,
                            their stalks are woven in baskets,
                    To-day we take the great breath of lovers,
                            to-morrow fate shuts us in.

Though you give all your kisses
                            you give but few.

Nor can I shift my pains to other,
        Hers will I be dead,
If she confer such nights upon me,
                        long is my life, long in years,
If she give me many,
        God am I for the time.

VIII

JOVE, be merciful to that unfortunate woman
Or an ornamental death will be held to your debit,
The time is come, the air heaves in torridity,
The dry earth pants against the canicular heat,
But this heat is not the root of the matter:
        She did not respect all the gods;
Such derelictions have destroyed other young ladies aforetime,
And what they swore in the cupboard
                  wind and wave scattered away.

Was Venus exacerbated by the existence of a comparable equal?
        Is the ornamental goddess full of envy?
Have you contempted Juno's Pelasgian temples,
        Have you denied Pallas good eyes?
Or is it my tongue that wrongs you
             with perpetual ascription of graces?
There comes, it seems, and at any rate
          through perils, (so many) and of a vexed life,
The gentler hour of an ultimate day.

Io mooed the first years with averted head,
        And now drinks Nile water like a god,
Ino in her young days fled pellmell out of Thebes,
        Andromeda was offered to a sea-serpent
           and respectably married to Perseus,
Callisto, disguised as a bear,
            wandered through the Arcadian prairies
        While a black veil was over her stars,
What if your fates are accelerated,
            your quiet hour put forward,
You may find interment pleasing,

You will say that you succumbed to a danger identical,
          charmingly identical, with Semele's,
And believe it, and she also will believe it,
          being expert from experience,

And amid all the gloried and storied beauties of Maeonia
There shall be none in a better seat, not

                             one denying your prestige,

Now you may bear fate's stroke unperturbed,
Or Jove, harsh as he is, may turn aside your ultimate day.
Old lecher, let not Juno get wind of the matter,
Or perhaps Juno herself will go under,

                  If the young lady is taken?

There will be, in any case, a stir on Olympus.

                         IX

                          1

THE twisted rhombs ceased their clamour of accompaniment;
The scorched laurel lay in the fire-dust;
The moon still declined to descend out of heaven,

But the black ominous owl hoot was audible.

And one raft bears our fates

                         on the veiled lake toward Avernus
Sails spread on Cerulean waters, I would shed tears for two;
I shall live, if she continue in life,

         If she dies, I shall go with her.
Great Zeus, save the woman,

                         or she will sit before your feet in a veil,
                         and tell out the long list of her troubles.

                          2

Persephone and Dis, Dis, have mercy upon her,
There are enough women in hell,

                         quite enough beautiful women,
Iope, and Tyro, and Pasiphae, and the formal girls of Achaia,
And out of Troad, and from the Campania,

Death has his tooth in the lot,

                             Avernus lusts for the lot of them,

Beauty is not eternal, no man has perennial fortune,

Slow foot, or swift foot, death delays but for a season.

3

My light, light of my eyes,

                             you are escaped from great peril,

Go back to Great Dian's dances bearing suitable gifts,

Pay up your vow of night watches

                             to Dian goddess of virgins,

And unto me also pay debt:

The ten nights of your company you have

                             promised me.

X

LIGHT, light of my eyes, at an exceeding late hour I was
    wandering,

And intoxicated,

                           and no servant was leading me,

And a minute crowd of small boys came from opposite,

                           I do not know what boys,

And I am afraid of numerical estimate,

And some of them shook little torches,

                         and others held onto arrows,

And the rest laid their chains upon me,

                     and they were naked, the lot of them,

And one of the lot was given to lust.

"That incensed female has consigned him to our pleasure."

So spoke. And the noose was over my neck.

And another said "Get him plumb in the middle!

    "Shove along there, shove along!"

And another broke in upon this:

                   "He thinks that we are not gods."

"And she has been waiting for the scoundrel,
                                    and in a new Sidonian night cap,
And with more than Arabian odours,
                                    God knows where he has been.
She could scarcely keep her eyes open
                                    enter that much for his bail.
                                    Get along now!"

We were coming near to the house,
                                    and they gave another yank to my cloak,
And it was morning, and I wanted to see if she was alone, and
    resting,
And Cynthia was alone in her bed.
                                    I was stupefied.
I had never seen her looking so beautiful,
                        No, not when she was tunick'd in purple.

Such aspect was presented to me, me recently emerged from my
    visions,
You will observe that pure form has its value.

"You are a very early inspector of mistresses.
"Do you think I have adopted your habits?"
            There were upon the bed no signs of a voluptuous
                encounter,
            No signs of a second incumbent.

She continued:
            "No incubus has crushed his body against me,
            "Though spirits are celebrated for adultery.
            "And I am going to the temple of Vesta . . . "
                        and so on.

Since that day I have had no pleasant nights.

XI

1

THE harsh facts of your levity!

                                          Many and many.

I am hung here, a scare-crow for lovers.

2

Escape! There is, O Idiot, no escape,
    Flee if you like into Ranaus,
                            desire will follow you thither,
Though you heave into the air upon the gilded Pegasean back,
Though you had the feathery sandals of Perseus
To lift you up through split air,
The high tracks of Hermes would not afford you shelter.

Amor stands upon you, Love drives upon lovers,
                        a heavy mass on free necks.

It is our eyes you flee, not the city,
You do nothing, you plot inane schemes against me,
Languidly you stretch out the snare
                  with which I am already familiar,

And yet again, and newly rumour strikes on my ears.

Rumours of you throughout the city,
                  and no good rumour among them.

"You should not believe hostile tongues.
       "Beauty is slander's cock-shy.
"All lovely women have known this,"
       "Your glory is not outblotted by venom,"
"Phoebus our witness, your hands are unspotted."

A foreign lover brought down Helen's kingdom
               and she was led back, living, home;
The Cytharean brought low by Mars' lechery
           reigns in respectable heavens, . . .

Oh, oh, and enough of this,
                              by dew-spread caverns,
The Muses clinging to the mossy ridges;
                              to the ledge of the rocks:
Zeus' clever rapes, in the old days,
                              combusted Semele's, of Io strayed.
Oh how the bird flew from Trojan rafters,
Ida has lain with a shepherd, she has slept between sheep.

                              Even there, no escape
Not the Hyrcanian seaboard, not in seeking the shore of Eos.

All things are forgiven for one night of your games. . . .
Though you walk in the Via Sacra, with a peacock's tail for a fan.

XII

WHO, who will be the next man to entrust his girl to a friend?
Love interferes with fidelities;
The gods have brought shame on their relatives;
Each man wants the pomegranate for himself;
Amiable and harmonious people are pushed incontinent into duels,
A Trojan and adulterous person came to Menelaus under the rites
        of hospitium,
And there was a case in Colchis, Jason and that woman in Colchis;
And besides, Lynceus,
                    you were drunk.

Could you endure such promiscuity?
                              She was not renowned for fidelity;
But to jab a knife in my vitals, to have passed on a swig of poison,
Preferable, my dear boy, my dear Lynceus,
Comrade, comrade of my life, of my purse, of my person;
But in one bed, in one bed alone, my dear Lynceus
        I deprecate your attendance;
I would ask a like boon of Jove.

And you write of Achelöus, who contended with Hercules,
You write of Adrastus' horses and the funeral rites of Achenor,
And you will not leave off imitating Aeschylus.
            Though you make a hash of Antimachus,
You think you are going to do Homer.
            And still a girl scorns the gods,
Of all these young women
                        not one has enquired the cause of the world,
Nor the modus of lunar eclipses
                        Nor whether there be any patch left of us
After we cross the infernal ripples,
                        nor if the thunder fall from predestination;
Nor anything else of importance.

Upon the Actian marshes Virgil is Phoebus' chief of police,
        He can tabulate Caesar's great ships.
He thrills to Ilian arms,
        He shakes the Trojan weapons of Aeneas,
And casts stores on Lavinian beaches.

Make way, ye Roman authors,
                        clear the street, O ye Greeks,
For a much larger Iliad is in the course of construction
(and to Imperial order)
Clear the streets, O ye Greeks!

And you also follow him "neath Phrygian pine shade:
        Thyrsis and Daphnis upon whittled reeds,
And how ten sins can corrupt young maidens;
        Kids for a bribe and pressed udders,
Happy selling poor loves for cheap apples.

Tityrus might have sung the same vixen;
        Corydon tempted Alexis,
Head farmers do likewise, and lying weary amid their oats
They get praise from tolerant Hamadryads."
Go on, to Ascraeus' prescription, the ancient,
                        respected, Wordsworthian:
"A flat field for rushes, grapes grow on the slope."

And behold me, small fortune left in my house.
Me, who had no general for a grandfather!
I shall triumph among young ladies of indeterminate character,
My talent acclaimed in their banquets,
        I shall be honoured with yesterday's wreaths.
And the god strikes to the marrow.

        Like a trained and performing tortoise,
I would make verse in your fashion, if she should command it,
With her husband asking a remission of sentence,
        And even this infamy would not attract numerous readers
Were there an erudite or violent passion,
For the nobleness of the populace brooks nothing below its own
    altitude.
One must have resonance, resonance and sonority . . . like a
    goose.

Varro sang Jason's expedition,
                Varro, of his great passion Leucadia,
There is song in the parchment; Catullus the highly indecorous,
Of Lesbia, known above Helen;
And in the dyed pages of Calvus,
        Calvus mourning Quintilia,
And but now Gallus had sung of Lycoris.
        Fair, fairest Lycoris—
The waters of Styx poured over the wound:
And now Propertius of Cynthia, taking his stand among these.

CANTUS PLANUS

THE black panther lies under his rose tree
And the fawns come to sniff at his sides:

Evoe, Evoe, Evoe Baccho, O
ZAGREUS, *Zagreus*, Zagreus,

The black panther lies under his rose tree.

‖ Hesper adest. Hesper ‖ adest.
Hesper ‖ adest. ‖

A DRAFT OF
XXX CANTOS

I

AND then went down to the ship,
Set keel to breakers, forth on the godly sea, and
We set up mast and sail on that swart ship,
Bore sheep aboard her, and our bodies also
Heavy with weeping, and winds from sternward
Bore us out onward with bellying canvas,
Circe's this craft, the trim-coifed goddess.
Then sat we amidships, wind jamming the tiller,
Thus with stretched sail, we went over sea till day's end.
Sun to his slumber, shadows o'er all the ocean,
Came we then to the bounds of deepest water,
To the Kimmerian lands, and peopled cities
Covered with close-webbed mist, unpierced ever
With glitter of sun-rays
Nor with stars stretched, nor looking back from heaven
Swartest night stretched over wretched men there.
The ocean flowing backward, came we then to the place
Aforesaid by Circe.
Here did they rites, Perimedes and Eurylochus,
And drawing sword from my hip
I dug the ell-square pitkin;
Poured we libations unto each the dead,
First mead and then sweet wine, water mixed with white flour.
Then prayed I many a prayer to the sickly death's-heads;
As set in Ithaca, sterile bulls of the best
For sacrifice, heaping the pyre with goods,
A sheep to Tiresias only, black and a bell-sheep.
Dark blood flowed in the fosse,
Souls out of Erebus, cadaverous dead, of brides
Of youths and of the old who had borne much;
Souls stained with recent tears, girls tender,
Men many, mauled with bronze lance heads,
Battle spoil, bearing yet dreory arms,
These many crowded about me; with shouting,
Pallor upon me, cried to my men for more beasts;

Slaughtered the herds, sheep slain of bronze;
Poured ointment, cried to the gods,
To Pluto the strong, and praised Proserpine;
Unsheathed the narrow sword,
I sat to keep off the impetuous impotent dead,
Till I should hear Tiresias.
But first Elpenor came, our friend Elpenor,
Unburied, cast on the wide earth,
Limbs that we left in the house of Circe,
Unwept, unwrapped in sepulchre, since toils urged other.
Pitiful spirit.   And I cried in hurried speech:
"Elpenor, how art thou come to this dark coast?
"Cam'st thou afoot, outstripping seamen?"
            And he in heavy speech:
"Ill fate and abundant wine.   I slept in Circe's ingle.
"Going down the long ladder unguarded,
"I fell against the buttress,
"Shattered the nape-nerve, the soul sought Avernus.
"But thou, O King, I bid remember me, unwept, unburied,
"Heap up mine arms, be tomb by sea-bord, and inscribed:
"*A man of no fortune, and with a name to come.*
"And set my oar up, that I swung mid fellows."

And Anticlea came, whom I beat off, and then Tiresias Theban,
Holding his golden wand, knew me, and spoke first:
"A second time? why? man of ill star,
"Facing the sunless dead and this joyless region?
"Stand from the fosse, leave me my bloody bever
"For soothsay."
            And I stepped back,
And he strong with the blood, said then: "Odysseus
"Shalt return through spiteful Neptune, over dark seas,
"Lose all companions."   And then Anticlea came.
Lie quiet Divus.   I mean, that is Andreas Divus,
In officina Wecheli, 1538, out of Homer.
And he sailed, by Sirens and thence outward and away
And unto Circe.
            Venerandam,

In the Cretan's phrase, with the golden crown, Aphrodite,
Cypri munimenta sortita est, mirthful, orichalchi, with golden
Girdles and breast bands, thou with dark eyelids
Bearing the golden bough of Argicida.   So that:

II

HANG it all, Robert Browning,
there can be but the one "Sordello."
But Sordello, and my Sordello?
Lo Sordels si fo di Mantovana.
So-shu churned in the sea.
Seal sports in the spray-whited circles of cliff-wash,
Sleek head, daughter of Lir,
            eyes of Picasso
Under black fur-hood, lithe daughter of Ocean;
And the wave runs in the beach-groove:
"Eleanor, ἐλέναυς and ἐλέπτολις!"
            And poor old Homer blind, blind, as a bat,
Ear, ear for the sea-surge, murmur of old men's voices:
"Let her go back to the ships,
Back among Grecian faces, lest evil come on our own,
Evil and further evil, and a curse cursed on our children,
Moves, yes she moves like a goddess
And has the face of a god
            and the voice of Schoeney's daughters,
And doom goes with her in walking,
Let her go back to the ships,
            back among Grecian voices."
And by the beach-run, Tyro,
            Twisted arms of the sea-god,
Lithe sinews of water, gripping her, cross-hold,
And the blue-gray glass of the wave tents them,
Glare azure of water, cold-welter, close cover.
Quiet sun-tawny sand-stretch,
The gulls broad out their wings,
            nipping between the splay feathers;
Snipe come for their bath,
            bend out their wing-joints,
Spread wet wings to the sun-film,
And by Scios,
            to left of the Naxos passage,

Naviform rock overgrown,
　　　algæ cling to its edge,
There is a wine-red glow in the shallows,
　　　a tin flash in the sun-dazzle.

The ship landed in Scios,
　　　men wanting spring-water,
And by the rock-pool a young boy loggy with vine-must,
　　　"To Naxos? Yes, we'll take you to Naxos,
Cum' along lad." "Not that way!"
"Aye, that way is Naxos."
　　　And I said: "It's a straight ship."
And an ex-convict out of Italy
　　　knocked me into the fore-stays,
(He was wanted for manslaughter in Tuscany)
　　　And the whole twenty against me,
Mad for a little slave money.
　　　And they took her out of Scios
And off her course...
　　　And the boy came to, again, with the racket,
And looked out over the bows,
　　　and to eastward, and to the Naxos passage.
God-sleight then, god-sleight:
　　　Ship stock fast in sea-swirl,
Ivy upon the oars, King Pentheus,
　　　grapes with no seed but sea-foam,
Ivy in scupper-hole.
Aye, I, Accœtes, stood there,
　　　and the god stood by me,
Water cutting under the keel,
Sea-break from stern forrards,
　　　wake running off from the bow,
And where was gunwale, there now was vine-trunk,
And tenthril where cordage had been,
　　　grape-leaves on the rowlocks,
Heavy vine on the oarshafts,

And, out of nothing, a breathing,
        hot breath on my ankles,
Beasts like shadows in glass,
        a furred tail upon nothingness.
Lynx-purr, and heathery smell of beasts,
        where tar smell had been,
Sniff and pad-foot of beasts,
        eye-glitter out of black air.
The sky overshot, dry, with no tempest,
Sniff and pad-foot of beasts,
        fur brushing my knee-skin,
Rustle of airy sheaths,
        dry forms in the *æther*.
And the ship like a keel in ship-yard,
        slung like an ox in smith's sling,
Ribs stuck fast in the ways,
        grape-cluster over pin-rack,
        void air taking pelt.
Lifeless air become sinewed,
        feline leisure of panthers,
Leopards sniffing the grape shoots by scupper-hole,
Crouched panthers by fore-hatch,
And the sea blue-deep about us,
        green-ruddy in shadows,
And Lyæus: "From now, Acœtes, my altars,
Fearing no bondage,
        fearing no cat of the wood,
Safe with my lynxes,
        feeding grapes to my leopards,
Olibanum is my incense,
        the vines grow in my homage."

The back-swell now smooth in the rudder-chains,
Black snout of a porpoise
        where Lycabs had been,
Fish-scales on the oarsmen.
        And I worship.

I have seen what I have seen.
   When they brought the boy I said:
"He has a god in him,
   though I do not know which god."
And they kicked me into the fore-stays.
I have seen what I have seen:
   Medon's face like the face of a dory,
Arms shrunk into fins. And you, Pentheus,
Had as well listen to Tiresias, and to Cadmus,
   or your luck will go out of you.
Fish-scales over groin muscles,
   lynx-purr amid sea...
And of a later year,
   pale in the wine-red algæ
If you will lean over the rock,
   the coral face under wave-tinge,
Rose-paleness under water-shift,
   Ileuthyeria, fair Dafne of sea-bords,
The swimmer's arms turned to branches,
Who will say in what year,
   fleeing what band of tritons,
The smooth brows, seen, and half seen,
   now ivory stillness.

And So-shu churned in the sea, So-shu also,
   using the long moon for a churn-stick...
Lithe turning of water,
   sinews of Poseidon,
Black azure and hyaline,
   glass wave over Tyro,
Close cover, unstillness,
   bright welter of wave-cords,
Then quiet water,
   quiet in the buff sands,
Sea-fowl stretching wing-joints,
   splashing in rock-hollows and sand-hollows
In the wave-runs by the half-dune;

Glass-glint of wave in the tide-rips against sunlight,
          pallor of Hesperus,
Grey peak of the wave,
          wave, colour of grape's pulp,

Olive grey in the near,
          far, smoke grey of the rock-slide,
Salmon-pink wings of the fish-hawk
          cast grey shadows in water,
The tower like a one-eyed great goose
          cranes up out of the olive-grove,

And we have heard the fauns chiding Proteus
          in the smell of hay under the olive-trees,
And the frogs singing against the fauns
          in the half-light.
And...

III

I SAT on the Dogana's steps
For the gondolas cost too much, that year,
And there were not "those girls," there was one face,
And the Buccentoro twenty yards off, howling "Stretti,"
And the lit cross-beams, that year, in the Morosini,
And peacocks in Koré's house, or there may have been.
          Gods float in the azure air,
Bright gods and Tuscan, back before dew was shed.
Light: and the first light, before ever dew was fallen.
Panisks, and from the oak, dryas,
And from the apple, mælid,
Through all the wood, and the leaves are full of voices,
A-whisper, and the clouds bowe over the lake,
And there are gods upon them,
And in the water, the almond-white swimmers,
The silvery water glazes the upturned nipple,
          As Poggio has remarked.
Green veins in the turquoise,
Or, the gray steps lead up under the cedars.

My Cid rode up to Burgos,
Up to the studded gate between two towers,
Beat with his lance butt, and the child came out,
Una niña de nueve años,
To the little gallery over the gate, between the towers,
Reading the writ, voce tinnula:
That no man speak to, feed, help Ruy Diaz,
On pain to have his heart out, set on a pike spike
And both his eyes torn out, and all his goods sequestered,
"And here, Myo Cid, are the seals,
The big seal and the writing."
And he came down from Bivar, Myo Cid,
With no hawks left there on their perches,
And no clothes there in the presses,
And left his trunk with Raquel and Vidas,
That big box of sand, with the pawn-brokers,

To get pay for his menie;
Breaking his way to Valencia.
Ignez da Castro murdered, and a wall
Here stripped, here made to stand.
Drear waste, the pigment flakes from the stone,
Or plaster flakes, Mantegna painted the wall.
Silk tatters, "Nec Spe Nec Metu."

IV

PALACE in smoky light,
Troy but a heap of smouldering boundary stones,
ANAXIFORMINGES!   Aurunculeia!
Hear me.   Cadmus of Golden Prows!
The silver mirrors catch the bright stones and flare,
Dawn, to our waking, drifts in the green cool light;
Dew-haze blurs, in the grass, pale ankles moving.
Beat, beat, whirr, thud, in the soft turf
            under the apple trees,
Choros nympharum, goat-foot, with the pale foot alternate;
Crescent of blue-shot waters, green-gold in the shallows,
A black cock crows in the sea-foam;

And by the curved, carved foot of the couch,
            claw-foot and lion head, an old man seated
Speaking in the low drone... :
                Ityn!
Et ter flebiliter, Ityn, Ityn!
And she went toward the window and cast her down,
        "All the while, the while, swallows crying:
Ityn!
        "It is Cabestan's heart in the dish."
        "It is Cabestan's heart in the dish?
        "No other taste shall change this."
And she went toward the window,
                the slim white stone bar
Making a double arch;
Firm even fingers held to the firm pale stone;
Swung for a moment,
                and the wind out of Rhodez
Caught in the full of her sleeve.
        . . . the swallows crying:
'Tis.   'Tis.   Ytis!
        Actæon...
            and a valley,
The valley is thick with leaves, with leaves, the trees,

The sunlight glitters, glitters a-top,
Like a fish-scale roof,
        Like the church roof in Poictiers
If it were gold.
        Beneath it, beneath it
Not a ray, not a slivver, not a spare disc of sunlight
Flaking the black, soft water;
Bathing the body of nymphs, of nymphs, and Diana,
Nymphs, white-gathered about her, and the air, air,
Shaking, air alight with the goddess,
        fanning their hair in the dark,
Lifting, lifting and waffing:
Ivory dipping in silver,
        Shadow'd, o'ershadow'd
Ivory dipping in silver,
Not a splotch, not a lost shatter of sunlight.
Then Actæon: Vidal,
Vidal.   It is old Vidal speaking,
        stumbling along in the wood,
Not a patch, not a lost shimmer of sunlight,
        the pale hair of the goddess.

The dogs leap on Actæon,
        "Hither, hither, Actæon,"
Spotted stag of the wood;
Gold, gold, a sheaf of hair,
        Thick like a wheat swath,
Blaze, blaze in the sun,
        The dogs leap on Actæon.
Stumbling, stumbling along in the wood,
Muttering, muttering Ovid:
        "Pergusa... pool... pool... Gargaphia,
"Pool... pool of Salmacis."
        The empty armour shakes as the cygnet moves.

Thus the light rains, thus pours, *e lo soleills plovil*
The liquid and rushing crystal
        beneath the knees of the gods.

Ply over ply, thin glitter of water;
Brook film bearing white petals.
The pine at Takasago
            grows with the pine of Isé!
The water whirls up the bright pale sand in the spring's mouth
"Behold the Tree of the Visages!"
Forked branch-tips, flaming as if with lotus.
            Ply over ply
The shallow eddying fluid,
            beneath the knees of the gods.

Torches melt in the glare
            set flame of the corner cook-stall,
Blue agate casing the sky (as at Gourdon that time)
            the sputter of resin,
Saffron sandal so petals the narrow foot: Hymenæus Io!
            Hymen, Io Hymenæe! Aurunculeia!
One scarlet flower is cast on the blanch-white stone.

            And Sō-Gyoku, saying:
"This wind, sire, is the king's wind,
            This wind is wind of the palace,
Shaking imperial water-jets."
            And Hsiang, opening his collar:
"This wind roars in the earth's bag,
            it lays the water with rushes."
No wind is the king's wind.
            Let every cow keep her calf.
"This wind is held in gauze curtains..."
            No wind is the king's...

The camel drivers sit in the turn of the stairs,
            Look down on Ecbatan of plotted streets,
"Danaë! Danaë!
            What wind is the king's?"
Smoke hangs on the stream,
The peach-trees shed bright leaves in the water,

Sound drifts in the evening haze,
　　　The bark scrapes at the ford,
Gilt rafters above black water,
　　　Three steps in an open field,
Gray stone-posts leading...

Père Henri Jacques would speak with the Sennin, on Rokku,
Mount Rokku between the rock and the cedars,
Polhonac,
As Gyges on Thracian platter set the feast,
Cabestan, Tereus,
　　　It is Cabestan's heart in the dish,
Vidal, or Ecbatan, upon the gilded tower in Ecbatan
Lay the god's bride, lay ever, waiting the golden rain.
By Garonne.   "Saave!"
The Garonne is thick like paint,
Procession,—"Et sa'ave, sa'ave, sa'ave Regina!"—
Moves like a worm, in the crowd.
Adige, thin film of images,
Across the Adige, by Stefano, Madonna in hortulo,
As Cavalcanti had seen her.
　　　The Centaur's heel plants in the earth loam.
And we sit here...
　　　there in the arena...

V

GREAT bulk, huge mass, thesaurus;
Ecbatan, the clock ticks and fades out
The bride awaiting the god's touch; Ecbatan,
City of patterned streets; again the vision:
Down in the viæ stradæ, toga'd the crowd, and arm'd,
Rushing on populous business,
and from parapet looked down
and North was Egypt,
   the celestial Nile, blue deep,
   cutting low barren land,
Old men and camels
      working the water-wheels;
Measureless seas and stars,
Iamblichus' light,
   the souls ascending,
Sparks like a partridge covey,
   Like the "ciocco," brand struck in the game.
"Et omniformis:" Air, fire, the pale soft light.
Topaz I manage, and three sorts of blue;
   but on the barb of time.
The fire? always, and the vision always,
Ear dull, perhaps, with the vision, flitting
And fading at will. Weaving with points of gold,
Gold-yellow, saffron... The roman shoe, Aurunculeia's
And come shuffling feet, and cries "Da nuces!
"Nuces!" praise, and Hymenæus "brings the girl to her man"
Or "here Sextus had seen her."
Titter of sound about me, always.
   and from "Hesperus..."
Hush of the older song: "Fades light from sea-crest,
"And in Lydia walks with pair'd women
"Peerless among the pairs, that once in Sardis
"In satieties...
   Fades the light from the sea, and many things
"Are set abroad and brought to mind of thee,"
And the vinestocks lie untended, new leaves come to the shoots,

North wind nips on the bough, and seas in heart
Toss up chill crests,
        And the vine stocks lie untended
And many things are set abroad and brought to mind
Of thee, Atthis, unfruitful.
        The talks ran long in the night.
And from Mauleon, fresh with a new earned grade,
In maze of approaching rain-steps, Poicebot—
The air was full of women,
        And Savairic Mauleon
Gave him his land and knight's fee, and he wed the woman.
Came lust of travel on him, of *romerya*;
And out of England a knight with slow-lifting eyelids
Lei fassa furar a del, put glamour upon her...
And left her an eight months gone.
        "Came lust of woman upon him,"
Poicebot, now on North road from Spain
(Sea-change, a grey in the water)
        And in small house by town's edge
Found a woman, changed and familiar face;
Hard night, and parting at morning.

And Pieire won the singing, Pieire de Maensac,
Song or land on the throw, and was *dreitz hom*
And had De Tierci's wife and with the war they made:
        Troy in Auvergnat
While Menelaus piled up the church at port
He kept Tyndarida.   Dauphin stood with de Maensac.

John Borgia is bathed at last. (Clock-tick pierces the vision)
Tiber, dark with the cloak, wet cat gleaming in patches.
Click of the hooves, through garbage,
Clutching the greasy stone. "And the cloak floated."
Slander is up betimes.
        But Varchi of Florence,
Steeped in a different year, and pondering Brutus,
Then "Σίγα μαλ' αὖθις δευτέραν!

"Dog-eye!!" (to Alessandro)
          "Whether for love of Florence," Varchi leaves it,
Saying "I saw the man, came up with him at Venice,
"I, one wanting the facts,
"And no mean labour...   Or for a privy spite?"
Our Benedetto leaves it,
But: "I saw the man. *Se pia?*
"*O empia?*   For Lorenzaccio had thought of stroke in the open
But uncertain (for the Duke went never unguarded)
"And would have thrown him from wall
"Yet feared this might not end him," or lest Alessandro
Know not by whom death came, O se credesse
"If when the foot slipped, when death came upon him,
"Lest cousin Duke Alessandro think he had fallen alone,
"No friend to aid him in falling."
                              Caina attende.
The lake of ice there below me.
And all of this, runs Varchi, dreamed out beforehand
In Perugia, caught in the star-maze by Del Carmine,
Cast on a natal paper, set with an exegesis, told,
All told to Alessandro, told thrice over,
Who held his death for a doom.
In abuleia.   But Don Lorenzino
Whether for love of Florence ... but
"O se morisse, credesse caduto da sè"
Σίγα, σίγα
Schiavoni, caught on the wood-barge,
Gives out the afterbirth, Giovanni Borgia,
Trails out no more at nights, where Barabello
Prods the Pope's elephant, and gets no crown, where Mozarello
Takes the Calabrian roadway, and for ending
Is smothered beneath a mule,
          a poet's ending,
Down a stale well-hole, oh a poet's ending.   "Sanazarro
"Alone out of all the court was faithful to him"
For the gossip of Naples' trouble drifts to North,
Fracastor (lightning was midwife) Cotta, and Ser D'Alviano,

Al poco giorno ed al gran cerchio d'ombra,
Talk the talks out with Navighero,
Burner of yearly Martials,
          (The slavelet is mourned in vain)
And the next comer says "Were nine wounds,
"Four men, white horse.   Held on the saddle before him..."
Hooves clink and slick on the cobbles.
Schiavoni... cloak... "Sink the damn thing!"
Splash wakes that chap on the wood-barge.
Tiber catching the nap, the moonlit velvet,
A wet cat gleaming in patches.
          "Se pia," Varchi,
"O empia, ma risoluto
"E terribile deliberazione."
          Both sayings run in the wind,
Ma se morisse!

VI

WHAT you have done, Odysseus,
      We know what you have done...
And that Guillaume sold out his ground rents
(Seventh of Poitiers, Ninth of Aquitain).
      "Tant las fotei com auzirets
      "Cen e quatre vingt et veit vetz..."
The stone is alive in my hand, the crops
      will be thick in my death-year...
Till Louis is wed with Eleanor
And had (He, Guillaume) a son that had to wife
The Duchess of Normandia whose daughter
Was wife to King Henry e maire del rei jove...
Went over sea till day's end (he, Louis, with Eleanor)
Coming at last to Acre.
"Ongla, oncle" saith Arnaut
    Her uncle commanded in Acre,
That had known her in girlhood
      (Theseus, son of Aegeus)
And he, Louis, was not at ease in that town,
And was not at ease by Jordan
As she rode out to the palm-grove
Her scarf in Saladin's cimier.
Divorced her in that year, he Louis,
      divorcing thus Aquitaine.
And that year Plantagenet married her
      (that had dodged past 17 suitors)
Et quand lo reis Lois lo entendit
      mout er fasché.
Nauphal, Vexis, Harry joven
In pledge for all his life and life of all his heirs
Shall have Gisors, and Vexis, Neufchastel
But if no issue Gisors shall revert...

"Need not wed Alix... in the name
Trinity holy indivisible... Richard our brother
Need not wed Alix once his father's ward and...
But whomso he choose... for Alix, etc...

Eleanor, domna jauzionda, mother of Richard,
Turning on thirty years (wd. have been years before this)
By river-marsh, by galleried church-porch,
Malemorte, Correze, to whom:
          "My Lady of Ventadour
"Is shut by Eblis in
"And will not hawk nor hunt
          nor get her free in the air
"Nor watch fish rise to bait
"Nor the glare-wing'd flies alight in the creek's edge
"Save in my absence, Madame.
          'Que la lauzeta mover'
"Send word I ask you to Eblis
          you have seen that maker
"And finder of songs so far afield as this
"That he may free her,
          who sheds such light in the air."

E lo Sordels si fo di Mantovana,
Son of a poor knight, Sier Escort,
And he delighted himself in chançons
And mixed with the men of the court
And went to the court of Richard Saint Boniface
And was there taken with love for his wife
                    Cunizza, da Romano,
That freed her slaves on a Wednesday
Masnatas et servos, witness
Picus de Farinatis
and Don Elinus and Don Lipus
          sons of Farinato de' Farinati

"free of person, free of will
"free to buy, witness, sell, testate."
A marito subtraxit ipsam...
          dictum Sordellum concubuisse:
          "Winter and Summer I sing of her grace,
          As the rose is fair, so fair is her face,

Both Summer and Winter I sing of her,
The snow makyth me to remember her."

And Cairels was of Sarlat...

Theseus from Troezene
And they wd. have given him poison
But for the shape of his sword-hilt.

ELEANOR (she spoiled in a British climate)
"Ελανδρος and 'Ελέπτολις, and
poor old Homer blind,
blind as a bat,
Ear, ear for the sea-surge;
            rattle of old men's voices.
And then the phantom Rome,
            marble narrow for seats
"Si pulvis nullus" said Ovid,
"Erit, nullum tamen excute."
Then file and candles, e li mestiers ecoutes;
Scene for the battle only, but still scene,
Pennons and standards y cavals armatz
Not mere succession of strokes, sightless narration,
And Dante's "ciocco," brand struck in the game.

Un peu moisi, plancher plus bas que le jardin.

"Contre le lambris, fauteuil de paille,
"Un vieux piano, et sous le baromètre..."

The old men's voices, beneath the columns of false marble,
The modish and darkish walls,
Discreeter gilding, and the panelled wood
Suggested, for the leasehold is
Touched with an imprecision... about three squares;
The house too thick, the paintings
a shade too oiled.
And the great domed head, *con gli occhi onesti e tardi*
Moves before me, phantom with weighted motion,
Grave incessu, drinking the tone of things,
And the old voice lifts itself
            weaving an endless sentence.

We also made ghostly visits, and the stair
That knew us, found us again on the turn of it,

Knocking at empty rooms, seeking for buried beauty;
And the sun-tanned, gracious and well-formed fingers
Lift no latch of bent bronze, no Empire handle
Twists for the knocker's fall; no voice to answer.
A strange concierge, in place of the gouty-footed.
Sceptic against all this one seeks the living,
Stubborn against the fact.   The wilted flowers
Brushed out a seven year since, of no effect.
Damn the partition!   Paper, dark brown and stretched,
Flimsy and damned partition.
      Ione, dead the long year
My lintel, and Liu Ch'e's lintel.
Time blacked out with the rubber.
      The Elysée carries a name on
And the bus behind me gives me a date for peg;
Low ceiling and the Erard and the silver,
These are in "time."   Four chairs, the bow-front dresser,
The panier of the desk, cloth top sunk in.
      "Beer-bottle on the statue's pediment!
"That, Fritz, is the era, to-day against the past,
"Contemporary."   And the passion endures.
Against their action, aromas.   Rooms, against chronicles.
Smaragdos, chrysolithos; De Gama wore striped pants in Africa
And "Mountains of the sea gave birth to troops";

Le vieux commode en acajou:
      beer-bottles of various strata,
But *is* she dead as Tyro?   In seven years?
Ελέναυς, ἕλανδρος, ἑλέπτολις
The sea runs in the beach-groove, shaking the floated pebbles,
Eleanor!
      The scarlet curtain throws a less scarlet shadow;
Lamplight at Buovilla, e quel remir,
      And all that day
Nicea moved before me
And the cold grey air troubled her not
For all her naked beauty, bit not the tropic skin,
And the long slender feet lit on the curb's marge

And her moving height went before me,
        We alone having being.
And all that day, another day:
        Thin husks I had known as men,
Dry casques of departed locusts
        speaking a shell of speech...
Propped between chairs and table...
Words like the locust-shells, moved by no inner being;
        A dryness calling for death;

Another day, between walls of a sham Mycenian,
"Toc" sphinxes, sham-Memphis columns,
And beneath the jazz a cortex, a stiffness or stillness,
        Shell of the older house.
Brown-yellow wood, and the no colour plaster,
Dry professorial talk...
        now stilling the ill beat music,
House expulsed by this house.

        Square even shoulders and the satin skin,
Gone cheeks of the dancing woman,
        Still the old dead dry talk, gassed out—
It is ten years gone, makes stiff about her a glass,
A petrefaction of air.
        The old room of the tawdry class asserts itself;
The young men, never!
        Only the husk of talk.
O voi che siete in piccioletta barca,
Dido choked up with sobs, for her Sicheus
Lies heavy in my arms, dead weight
        Drowning, with tears, new Eros,

And the life goes on, mooning upon bare hills;
Flame leaps from the hand, the rain is listless,
Yet drinks the thirst from our lips,
        solid as echo,
Passion to breed a form in shimmer of rain-blur;

But Eros drowned, drowned, heavy-half dead with tears
        For dead Sicheus.

Life to make mock of motion:
For the husks, before me, move,
        The words rattle: shells given out by shells.
The live man, out of lands and prisons,
        shakes the dry pods,
Probes for old wills and friendships, and the big locust-casques
Bend to the tawdry table,
Lift up their spoons to mouths, put forks in cutlets,
And make sound like the sound of voices.
        Lorenzaccio
Being more live than they, more full of flames and voices.
Ma se morisse!
        Credesse caduto da sè, ma se morisse.
And the tall indifference moves,
        a more living shell,
Drift in the air of fate, dry phantom, but intact.
O Alessandro, chief and thrice warned, watcher,
        Eternal watcher of things,
Of things, of men, of passions.
        Eyes floating in dry, dark air,
E biondo, with glass-grey iris, with an even side-fall of hair
The stiff, still features.

VIII

THESE fragments you have shelved (shored).
    "Slut!" "Bitch!" Truth and Calliope
Slanging each other sous les lauriers:
That Alessandro was negroid. And Malatesta
Sigismund:
        Frater tamquam
Et compater carissime: tergo
                ...hanni de
                ..dicis
                ...entia
Equivalent to:
            Giohanni of the Medici,
            Florence,
Letter received, and in the matter of our Messire Gianozio,
One from him also, sent on in form and with all due dispatch,
Having added your wishes and memoranda.
As to arranging peace between you and the King of Ragona,
So far as I am concerned, it wd.
Give me the greatest possible pleasure,
At any rate nothing wd. give me more pleasure
    or be more acceptable to me,
And I shd. like to be party to it, as was promised me,
        either as participant or adherent.
As for my service money,
Perhaps you and your father wd. draw it
And send it on to me as quickly as possible.
And tell the *Maestro di pentore*
That there can be no question of
His painting the walls for the moment,
As the mortar is not yet dry
And it wd. be merely work chucked away
        (*buttato via*)
But I want it to be quite clear, that until the chapels are ready
I will arrange for him to paint something else
So that both he and I shall
Get as much enjoyment as possible from it,

And in order that he may enter my service
And also because you write me that he needs cash,
I want to arrange with him to give him so much per year
And to assure him that he will get the sum agreed on.
You may say that I will deposit security
For him wherever he likes.
And let me have a clear answer,
For I mean to give him good treatment
So that he may come to live the rest
Of his life in my lands—
Unless you put him off it—
And for this I mean to make due provision,
So that he can work as he likes,
Or waste his time as he likes
(*affatigandose per suo piacere o no
non gli manchera la provixione mai*)
                                        never lacking provision.
          SIGISMUNDUS PANDOLPHUS DE MALATESTIS
          *In campo Illus. Domini Venetorum die 7
          aprilis* 1449 *contra Cremonam*

      . . . . . and because the aforesaid most illustrious
Duke of Milan
Is content and wills that the aforesaid Lord Sigismundo
Go into the service of the most magnificent commune
of the Florentines
For alliance defensive of the two states,
Therefore between the aforesaid Illustrious Sigismund
And the respectable man Agnolo della Stufa,
                    ambassador, sindic and procurator
Appointed by the ten of the baily, etc., the half
Of these 50,000 florins, free of attainder,
For 1400 cavalry and four hundred foot
To come into the terrene of the commune
                    or elsewhere in Tuscany
As please the ten of the Baily,
And to be himself there with them in the service
of the commune

With his horsemen and his footmen
                    (*gente di cavallo e da pie*) etc.
                    Aug. 5 1452, *register of the Ten of the Baily.*

From the forked rocks of Penna and Billi, on Carpegna
with the road leading under the cliff,
                    in the wind-shelter into Tuscany,
And the north road, toward the Marecchia
                    the mud-stretch full of cobbles.
Lyra:
"Ye spirits who of olde were in this land
Each under Love, and shaken,
Go with your lutes, awaken
The summer within her mind,
Who hath not Helen for peer
                    Yseut nor Batsabe."
With the interruption:
                    Magnifico, compater et carissime
                    (Johanni di Cosimo)
Venice has taken me on again
                    At 7,000 a month, *fiorini di Camera.*
For 2,000 horse and four hundred footmen,
And it rains here by the gallon,
We have had to dig a new ditch.
In three or four days
I shall try to set up the bombards.

Under the plumes, with the flakes and small wads of colour
Showering from the balconies
With the sheets spread from windows,
                    with leaves and small branches pinned on them,
Arras hung from the railings; out of the dust,
With pheasant tails upright on their forelocks,
                    The small white horses, the
Twelve girls riding in order, green satin in pannier'd habits;
Under the baldachino, silver'd with heavy stitches,
Bianca Visconti, with Sforza,
The peasant's son and the duchess,

To Rimini, and to the wars southward,
Boats drawn on the sand, red-orange sails in the creek's mouth,
For two days' pleasure, mostly "*la pesca*," fishing,
Di cui in the which he, Francesco, *godeva molto.*
       To the war southward
In which he, at that time, received an excellent hiding.
And the Greek emperor was in Florence
       (Ferrara having the pest)
And with him Gemisthus Plethon
Talking of the war about the temple at Delphos,
And of POSEIDON, *concret Allgemeine,*
And telling of how Plato went to Dionysius of Syracuse
Because he had observed that tyrants
Were most efficient in all that they set their hands to,
But he was unable to persuade Dionysius
To any amelioration.
And in the gate at Ancona, between the foregate
And the main-gates
Sigismundo, ally, come through an enemy force,
To patch up some sort of treaty, passes one gate
And they shut it before they open the next gate, and he says:
"Now you have me,
       Caught like a hen in a coop."
And the captain of the watch says: "Yes Messire Sigismundo,
But we want this town for ourselves."

       With the church against him,
With the Medici bank for itself,
With wattle Sforza against him
Sforza Francesco, wattle-nose,
Who married him (Sigismundo) his (Francesco's)
Daughter in September,
Who stole Pèsaro in October (as Broglio says "*bestialmente*"),
Who stood with the Venetians in November,
With the Milanese in December,
Sold Milan in November, stole Milan in December
Or something of that sort,
Commanded the Milanese in the spring,

the Venetians at midsummer,
The Milanese in the autumn,
And was Naples' ally in October,
        He, Sigismundo, *templum ædificavit*
In Romagna, teeming with cattle thieves,
        with the game lost in mid-channel,
And never quite lost till '50,
        and never quite lost till the end, in Romagna,
So that Galeaz sold Pèsaro "to get pay for his cattle."

And Poictiers, you know, Guillaume Poictiers,
        had brought the song up out of Spain
With the singers and viels.   But here they wanted a setting,
By Marecchia, where the water comes down over the cobbles
And Mastin had come to Verucchio,
        and the sword, Paolo il Bello's,
        caught in the arras
And, in Este's house, Parisina
Paid
For this tribe paid always, and the house
Called also Atreides',
And the wind is still for a little
And the dusk rolled
        to one side a little
And he was twelve at the time, Sigismundo,
And no dues had been paid for three years,
And his elder brother gone pious;
And that year they fought in the streets,
And that year he got out to Cesena
        And brought back the levies,
And that year he crossed by night over Foglia, and...

IX

ONE year floods rose,
One year they fought in the snows,
One year hail fell, breaking the trees and walls.
Down here in the marsh they trapped him in one year,
And he stood in the water up to his neck
        to keep the hounds off him,
And he floundered about in the marsh
        and came in after three days,
That was Astorre Manfredi of Faenza
        who worked the ambush
        and set the dogs off to find him,
In the marsh, down here under Mantua,
And he fought in Fano, in a street fight,
        and that was nearly the end of him;
And the Emperor came down and knighted us,
And they had a wooden castle set up for fiesta,
And one year Basinio went out into the courtyard
        Where the lists were, and the palisades
        had been set for the tourneys,
And he talked down the anti-Hellene,
        And there was an heir male to the seignor,
        And Madame Ginevra died.
And he, Sigismundo, was Capitan for the Venetians.
And he had sold off small castles
        and built the great Rocca to his plan,
And he fought like ten devils at Monteluro
        and got nothing but the victory
And old Sforza bitched us at Pesaro;
        (sic) March the 16th:
"that Messire Alessandro Sforza
        is become lord of Pesaro
through the wangle of the Illus. Sgr. Mr. Fedricho d'Orbino
Who worked the wangle with Galeaz
        through the wiggling of Messer Francesco,
Who waggled it so that Galeaz should sell Pesaro
        to Alex and Fossembrone to Feddy;
and he hadn't the right to sell.

And this he did *bestialmente*; that is Sforza did *bestialmente*
as he had promised him, Sigismundo, *per capitoli*
      to see that he, Malatesta, should have Pesaro"
And this cut us off from our south half
      and finished our game, thus, in the beginning,
And he, Sigismundo, spoke his mind to Francesco
      and we drove them out of the Marches.

And the King o' Ragona, Alphonse le roy d'Aragon,
      was the next nail in our coffin,
And all you can say is, anyway,
that he Sigismundo called a town council
And Valturio said "as well for a sheep as a lamb"
      and this change-over (*hæc traditio*)
As old bladder said "*rem eorum saluavit*"
Saved the Florentine state; and that, maybe, was something.
And "Florence our natural ally" as they said in the meeting
      for whatever that was worth afterward.
And he began building the TEMPIO,
      and Polixena, his second wife, died.
And the Venetians sent down an ambassador
And said "speak humanely,
But tell him it's no time for raising his pay."
And the Venetians sent down an ambassador
      with three pages of secret instructions
To the effect: Did he think the campaign was a joy-ride?
And old Wattle-wattle slipped into Milan
But he couldn't stand Sidg being so high with the Venetians
And he talked it over with Feddy; and Feddy said "Pesaro"
And old Foscari wrote "*Caro mio*
"If we split with Francesco you can have it
"And we'll help you in every way possible."
      But Feddy offered it sooner.
And Sigismundo got up a few arches,
And stole that marble in Classe, "stole" that is,
Casus est talis:
      Foscari doge, to the prefect of Ravenna
"Why, what, which, thunder, damnation????"

Casus est talis:
   Filippo, commendatary of the abbazia
Of Sant Apollinaire, Class, Cardinal of Bologna
That he did one night (*quadam nocte*) sell to the
Ill^(mo) D°, D° Sigismund Malatesta
Lord of Arimininum, marble, porphyry, serpentine,
Whose men, Sigismundo's, came with more than an hundred
two wheeled ox carts and deported, for the beautifying
of the *tempio* where was Santa Maria in Trivio
Where the same are now on the walls. Four hundred
ducats to be paid back to the *abbazia* by the said swindling
Cardinal or his heirs.
   grnnh! rrnnh, pthg.
wheels, plaustra, oxen under night-shield,
And on the 13th of August: Aloysius Purtheo,
The next abbot, to Sigismundo, receipt for 200 ducats
Corn-salve for the damage done in that scurry.

And there was the row about that German-Burgundian female
And it was his messianic year, Poliorcetes,
   but he was being a bit too POLUMETIS
And the Venetians wouldn't give him six months vacation.

And he went down to the old brick heap of Pesaro
   and waited for Feddy
And Feddy finally said "I am coming!...
   ...to help Alessandro."
And he said: "This time Mister Feddy has done it."
He said: "Broglio, I'm the goat. This time
   Mr. Feddy has done it (*m'l'ha calata*)."
And he'd lost his job with the Venetians,
And the stone didn't come in from Istria:
And we sent men to the silk war;
And Wattle never paid up on the nail
   Though we signed on with Milan and Florence;
And he set up the bombards in muck down by Vada
   where nobody else could have set 'em
   and he took the wood out of the bombs

and made 'em of two scoops of metal
And the jobs getting smaller and smaller,
        Until he signed on with Siena;
        And that time they grabbed his post-bag.
And what was it, anyhow?
        Pitigliano, a man with a ten acre lot,
Two lumps of tufa,
        and they'd taken his pasture land from him,
And Sidg had got back their horses,
        and he had two big lumps of tufa
        with six hundred pigs in the basements.
And the poor devils were dying of cold.
And this is what they found in the post-bag:
            Ex Arimino die xxii Decembris
    "*Magnifice ac potens domine, mi singularissime*
"I advise yr. Lordship how
"I have been with master Alwidge who
"has shown me the design of the nave that goes in the middle,
"of the church and the design for the roof and..."
"JHesus,
"*Magnifico exso.*   Signor Mio
"Sence to-day I am recommanded that I have to tel you my father's
"opinium that he has shode to Mr. Genare about the valts of the
"cherch... etc ...
    "Giovane of Master alwise P. S.   I think it advisabl that I shud go
"to rome to talk to mister Albert so as I can no what he thinks about
"it rite.

"Sagramoro..."

"*Illustre signor mio*, Messire Battista..."

"First: Ten slabs best red, seven by 15, by one third,
"Eight ditto, good red, 15 by three by one,
"Six of same, 15 by one by one.
"Eight columns 15 by three and one third
            etc... with carriage, danars 151

"Monseigneur:

"Madame Isotta has had me write today about Sr. Galeazzo's
"daughter. The man who said young pullets make thin soup, knew
"what he was talking about. We went to see the girl the other day,
"for all the good that did, and she denied the whole matter and kept
"her end up without losing her temper. I think Madame Ixotta
"very nearly exhausted the matter. *Mi pare che avea decto hogni
"chossia*. All the children are well. Where you are everyone is
"pleased and happy because of your taking the chateau here we are
"the reverse as you might say drifting without a rudder. Madame
"Lucrezia has probably, or should have, written to you, I suppose
"you have the letter by now. Everyone wants to be remembered to
"you.   21 Dec. D. de M."

"... *sagramoro* to put up the derricks. There is a supply of beams
"at..."

"Magnificent lord with due reverence:

"Messire Malatesta is well and asks for you every day. He is so
"much pleased with his pony, It wd. take me a month to write you
"all the fun he gets out of that pony. I want to again remind you
"to write to Georgio Rambottom or to his boss to fix up that wall to
"the little garden that madame Isotta uses, for it is all flat on the
"ground now as I have already told him a lot of times, for all the
"good that does, so I am writing to your lordship in the matter I
"have done all that I can, for all the good that does as noboddy hear
"can do anything without you.
                       "your faithful
                                 Lunarda da Palla.
                                 20 Dec. 1454."

"... gone over it with all the foremen and engineers. And about
"the silver for the small medal..."

"*Magnifice ac potens*...
         "because the walls of..."

"*Malatesta de Malatestis ad Magnificum Dominum Patremque
"suum*.

"Ex^{so} D^{no} et D^{no} sin D^{no} Sigismundum Pandolfi Filium
      "Malatestis Capitan General

"Magnificent and Exalted Lord and Father in especial my lord with
"due recommendation: your letter has been presented to me by
"Gentilino da Gradara and with it the bay pony (ronzino baiectino)
"the which you have sent me, and which appears in my eyes a fine
"caparison'd charger, upon which I intend to learn all there is to
"know about riding, in consideration of yr. paternal affection for
"which I thank your excellency thus briefly and pray you continue
"to hold me in this esteem notifying you by the bearer of this that
"we are all in good health, as I hope and desire your Ex^{ct} Lordship
"is also: with continued remembrance I remain
            "Your son and servant
                  MALATESTA DE MALATESTIS.
      *Given in Rimini, this the 22nd day of December
                  anno domini 1454*"
            (*in the sixth year of his age*)

"ILLUSTRIOUS PRINCE:
    "Unfitting as it is that I should offer counsels to Hannibal..."

    "*Magnifice ac potens domine, domine mi singularissime, hu-*
"*mili recomendatione premissa* etc. This to advise your M^{gt} Ld^{shp}
"how the second load of Veronese marble has finally got here, after
"being held up at Ferrara with no end of fuss and botheration, the
"whole of it having been there unloaded.
    "I learned how it happened, and it has cost a few florins to get
"back the said load which had been seized for the skipper's debt and
"defalcation; he having fled when the lighter was seized.   But that
"Y^r M^{gt} Ld^{shp} may not lose the moneys paid out on his account I
"have had the lighter brought here and am holding it, against his
"arrival.   If not we still have the lighter.
    "As soon as the Xmas fêtes are over I will have the stone floor laid
"in the sacresty, for which the stone is already cut. The wall of the
"building is finished and I shall now get the roof on.
    "We have not begun putting new stone into the martyr chapel;
"first because the heavy frosts wd. certainly spoil the job; secondly

"because the aliofants aren't yet here and one can't get the measure-
"ments for the cornice to the columns that are to rest on the alio-
"fants.

"They are doing the stairs to your room in the castle... I have
"had Messire Antonio degli Atti's court paved and the stone benches
"put in it.

"Ottavian is illuminating the bull. I mean the bull for the cha-
"pel. All the stone-cutters are waiting for spring weather to start
"work again.

"The tomb is all done except part of the lid, and as soon as Mes-
"sire Agostino gets back from Cesena I will see that he finishes it,
"ever recommending me to y^r M^{gt} Ld^{shp}

"believe me y^r faithful
PETRUS GENARIIS."

That's what they found in the post-bag
And some more of it to the effect that
he "lived and ruled"

"*et amava perdutamente Ixotta degli Atti*"
e "*ne fu degna*"
"*constans in proposito*
"*Placuit oculis principis*
"*pulchra aspectu*"
"*populo grata (Italiaeque decus)*
"and built a temple so full of pagan works"
i. e. Sigismund
and in the style "Past ruin'd Latium"
The filigree hiding the gothic,
with a touch of rhetoric in the whole
And the old sarcophagi,
such as lie, smothered in grass, by San Vitale.

X

AND the poor devils dying of cold, outside Sorano,
And from the other side, from inside the château,
Orsini, Count Pitigliano, on the 17th of November:
"Siggy, darlint, wd. you not stop making war on insensible objects,
"such as trees and domestic vines, that have no means to hit back...
"but if you will hire yourself out to a commune (Siena) which you
"ought rather to rule than serve..."
            which with Trachulo's damn'd epistle...
And what of it *any*how? a man with a ten acre lot,
Pitigliano... a lump of tufa,
            And S. had got back their horses
And the poor devils dying of cold...
(And there was another time, you know,
He signed on with the Fanesi,
            and just couldn't be bothered...)
And there were three men on a one man job
            And Careggi wanting the baton,
And not getting it just then in any case.

And he, Sigismundo, refused an invitation to lunch
            In commemoration of Carmagnola
            (vide Venice, between the two columns
            where Carmagnola was executed.)
            Et
            "*anno messo a saccho el signor Sigismundo*"
As Filippo Strozzi wrote to Zan Lottieri, then in Naples,
            "I think they'll let him through at Campiglia"

            Florence, Archivio Storico, 4th Series t. iii, e
            "*La Guerra dei Senesi col conte di Pitigliano.*"

And he found Carlo Gonzaga sitting like a mud-frog
            in Orbetello
And he said:
            "*Caro mio,* I can not receive you
It really *is* not the moment."

And Broglio says he ought to have tipped Gorro Lolli.
But he got back home here somehow,
And Piccinino was out of a job,
And the old row with Naples continued.
And what he said was all right in Mantua;
And Borso had the pair of them up to Bel Fiore,
The pair of them, Sigismundo and Federico Urbino,
Or perhaps in the palace, Ferrara, Sigismund upstairs
And Urbino's gang in the basement,
And a regiment of guards in, to keep order,
          For all the good that did:
"*Te cavero la budella del corpo!*"
El conte levatosi:
          "*Io te cavero la corata a te!*"
And that day Cosimo smiled,
That is, the day they said:
          "Drusiana is to marry Count Giacomo..."
(Piccinino) *un sorriso malizioso.*
Drusiana, another of Franco Sforza's;
It would at least keep the row out of Tuscany.
And he fell out of a window, Count Giacomo,
Three days after his death, that was years later in Naples,
For trusting Ferdinando of Naples,
And old Wattle could do nothing about it.

                    Et:
....

INTEREA PRO GRADIBUS BASILICAE S. PIETRI EX ARIDA MATERIA INGENS
PYRA EXTRUITUR IN CUJUS SUMMITATE IMAGO SIGISMUNDI COLLO-
CATUR HOMINIS LINEAMENTA, ET VESTIMENTI MODUM ADEO PROPRIE
REDDENS, UT VERA MAGIS PERSONA, QUAM IMAGO VIDERETUR; NE
QUEM TAMEN IMAGO FALLERET, ET SCRIPTURA EX ORE PRODIIT, QUAE
DICERET:
          SIGISMUNDUS HIC EGO SUM
MALATESTA, FILIUS PANDULPHI, REX PRODITORUM,
DEO ATQUE HOMINIBUS INFESTUS, SACRI CENSURA SENATUS IGNI DAM-
NATUS;

                                        SCRIPTURAM

MULTI LEGERUNT. DEINDE ASTANTE POPULO, IGNE IMMISSO, ET PYRA
SIMULACRUM REPENTE FLAGRAVIT.

Com. Pio II, Liv. VII, p. 85.
Yriarte, p. 288.

....

So that in the end that pot-scraping little runt Andreas
      Benzi, da Siena
Got up to spout out the bunkum
That that monstrous swollen, swelling s. o. b.
      Papa Pio Secundo
      Æneas Silvius Piccolomini
      da Siena
Had told him to spout, in their best bear's-greased latinity;

Stupro, cæde, adulter,
homocidia, parricidia ac periurus,
presbitericidia, audax, libidinosus,
wives, jew-girls, nuns, necrophiliast, *fornicarium ac sicarium,*
proditor, raptor, incestuosus, incendiarius, ac
concubinarius,
and that he rejected the whole symbol of the apostles,
and that he said the monks ought not to own property
and that he disbelieved in the temporal power,
neither christian, jew, gentile,
      nor any sect pagan, *nisi forsitan epicureæ.*

And that he did among other things
Empty the fonts of the chiexa of holy water
And fill up the same full with ink
That he might in God's dishonour
Stand before the doors of the said chiexa
Making mock of the inky faithful, they
Issuing thence by the doors in the pale light of the sunrise
Which might be considered youthful levity
      but was really a profound indication;

"Whence that his, Sigismundo's, fœtor filled the earth
And stank up through the air and stars to heaven
Where—save they were immune from sufferings—
It had made the emparadisèd spirits pewk"
        from their jeweled terrace.

"*Lussurioso incestuoso, perfide, sozzure ac crapulone,
assassino, ingordo, avaro, superbo, infidele
fattore di monete false, sodomitico, uxoricido*"

and the whole lump lot
given over to...

I mean after Pio had said, or at least Pio says that he
Said that this was elegant oratory "*Orationem
Elegantissimam et ornatissimam
Audivimus venerabilis in Xti fratres ac dilectissimi
filii*... (stone in his bladder
        testibus idoneis)
The lump lot given over
To that kid-slapping fanatic il cardinale di San Pietro in Vincoli
        To find him guilty, of the lump lot
As he duly did, calling rumour, and Messire Federico d'Urbino
And other equally unimpeachable witnesses.

So they burnt our brother in effigy
A rare magnificent effigy costing 8 florins 48 bol
(i.e. for the pair, as the first one wasn't a good enough likeness)
And Borso said the time was ill-suited
        to *tanta novità*, such doings or innovations,
God's enemy and man's enemy, *stuprum, raptum*
        I. N. R. I. Sigismund Imperator, Rex Proditorum.

And old Pills who tried to get him into a front rank action
In order to drive the rear guard at his buttocks,
Old Pills listed among the murdered, although he
Came out of jail living later.

Et les angloys ne povans desraciner... venin de hayne
Had got back Gisors from the Angevins,

And the Angevins were gunning after Naples
And we dragged in the Angevins,
And we dragged in Louis Eleventh,
And the *tiers Calixte* was dead, and Alfonso;
And against us we had "this Æneas" and young Ferdinando
That we had smashed at Piombino and driven out of the
Terrene of the Florentines;
And Piccinino, out of a job;
And he, Sidg, had had three chances of
Making it up with Alfonso, and an offer of
Marriage alliance;

And what he said was all right there in Mantua;
But Pio, sometime or other, Pio lost his pustulous temper.
And they struck alum at Tolfa, in the pope's land,
        To pay for their devilment.
And Francesco said:
        I also have suffered.
When you take it, give me a slice.
        And they nearly jailed a chap for saying
The job was *mal hecho*; and they caught poor old Pasti
In Venice, and were like to pull all his teeth out;
And they had a bow-shot at Borso
As he was going down the Grand Canal in his gondola
        (the nice kind with 26 barbs on it)
And they said: Novvy'll sell any man
        for the sake of Count Giacomo.
(Piccinino, the one that fell out of the window).

And they came at us with their ecclesiastical legates
Until the eagle lit on his tent pole.
And he said: The Romans would have called that an augury

E gradment li antichi cavaler romanj
         davano fed a quisti annutii,
All I want you to do is to follow the orders,
They've got a bigger army,
         but there are more men in this camp.

XI

EGRADMENT *li antichi cavaler romanj*
          davano fed a quisti annutii
And he puts us under the chiefs,
          and the chiefs went back to their squadrons:
Bernardo Reggio, Nic Benzo, Giovan Nestorno,
Paulo Viterbo, Buardino of Brescia,
          Cetho Brandolino,
And Simone Malespina, Petracco Saint Archangelo,
Rioberto da Canossa,
And for the tenth Agniolo da Roma
          And that gay bird Piero della Bella,
And to the eleventh Roberto,
And the papishes were three thousand on horses,
dilly cavalli tre milia,
And a thousand on foot,
And the Lord Sigismundo had but mille tre cento cavalli
And hardly 500 fanti (and one spingard),
And we beat the papishes and fought
them back through the tents
And he came up to the dyke again
And fought through the dyke-gate
And it went on from dawn to sunset
And we broke them and took their baggage
          and mille cinquecento cavalli
E li homini di Messire Sigismundo
non furono che mille trecento

And the Venetians sent in their compliments
And various and sundry sent in their compliments;
But we got it next August;
And Roberto got beaten at Fano,
And he went by ship to Tarentum,
I mean Sidg went to Tarentum
And he found 'em, the anti-Aragons,
          busted and weeping into their beards.

And they, the papishes, came up to the walls,
And that nick-nosed s.o.b. Feddy Urbino
Said: *"Par che è fuor di questo... Sigis... mundo.""*
"They say he dodders about the streets
"And can put his hand to neither one thing nor the other,"
And he was in the sick wards, and on the high tower
And everywhere, keeping us at it.
And, thank God, they got the sickness outside
As we had the sickness inside,
And they had neither town nor castello
But dey got de mos' bloody rottenes' peace on us—
Quali lochi sono questi:
        Sogliano,
Torrano and La Serra, Sbrigara, San Martino,
Ciola, Pondo, Spinello, Cigna and Buchio,
Prataline, Monte Cogruzzo,
        and the villa at Rufiano
Right up to the door-yard
And anything else the Rev^mo Monsignore could remember.
And the water-rights on the Savio.
(And the salt heaps with the reed mats on them
        Gone long ago to the Venetians)
And when lame Novvy died, they got even Cesena.

And he wrote to young Piero:
        Send me a couple of huntin' dogs,
They may take my mind off it.
And one day he was sitting in the chiexa,
On a bit of cornice, a bit of stone grooved for a cornice,
Too narrow to fit his big beam,
        hunched up and noting what was done wrong,
And an old woman came in and giggled to see him
        sitting there in the dark
She nearly fell over him,
        And he thought:
Old Zuliano is finished,
If he's left anything we must see the kids get it,

Write that to Robert.
And Vanni must give that peasant a decent price for his horses,
Say that I will refund.

And the writs run in Fano,
For the long room over the arches
Sub annulo piscatoris, palatium seu curiam OLIM *de Malatestis.*
Gone, and Cesena, Zezena *d"e b"e colonne,*
And the big diamond pawned in Venice,
And he gone out into Morea,
Where they sent him to do in the Mo'ammeds,
With 5,000 against 25,000,
        and he nearly died out in Sparta,
Morea, Lakedæmon,
        and came back with no pep in him
And we sit here.   I have sat here
        For forty four thousand years,
And they trapped him down here in the marsh land,
        in '46 that was;
And the poor devils dying of cold, that was Rocca Sorano;
And he said in his young youth:
        Vogliamo,
che le donne, we will that they, *le donne,* go ornate,
As be their pleasure, for the city's glory thereby.

And Platina said afterward,
        when they jailed him
And the Accademia Romana,
For singing to Zeus in the catacombs,
Yes, I saw him when he was down here
Ready to murder fatty Barbo, "Formosus,"
And they want to know what we talked about?
        "*de litteris et de armis, praestantibusque ingeniis,*
Both of ancient times and our own; books, arms,
And of men of unusual genius,
Both of ancient times and our own, in short the usual subjects
Of conversation between intelligent men."

And he with his luck gone out of him
64 lances in his company, and his pay 8,000 a *year*,
64 and no more, and he not to try to get any more
And all of it down on paper
sexaginta quatuor nec tentatur habere plures
But leave to keep 'em in Rimini
        i.e. to watch the Venetians.

Damn pity he didn't
        (i.e. get the knife into him)
Little fat squab "Formosus"
Barbo said "Call me Formosus"
But the conclave wouldn't have it
        and they called him Paolo Secondo.

And he left three horses at one gate
        And three horses at the other,
And Fatty received him
        with a guard of seven cardinals "whom he could trust."
And the castelan of Montefiore wrote down,
"You'd better keep him out of the district.
"When he got back here from Sparta, the people
"Lit fires, and turned out yelling: 'PANDOLFO'!"

In the gloom, the gold gathers the light against it.
    And one day he said: Henry, you can have it,
On condition, you can have it: for four months
You'll stand any reasonable joke that I play on you,
And you can joke back
        provided you don't get too ornry.
And they put it all down in writing:
For a green cloak with silver brocade
Actum in Castro Sigismundo, presente Roberto de Valturibus
.. sponte et ex certa scienta... to Enricho de Aquabello.

XII

AND we sit here
        under the wall,
Arena romana, Diocletian's, les gradins
        quarante-trois rangées en calcaire.
Baldy Bacon
        bought all the little copper pennies in Cuba:
Un centavo, dos centavos,
        told his peons to "bring 'em in."
"Bring 'em to the main shack," said Baldy,
And the peons brought 'em;
"to the main shack brought 'em,"
As Henry would have said.
        Nicholas Castano in Habana,
He also had a few centavos, but the others
Had to pay a percentage.
        Percentage when they wanted centavos,
Public centavos.
        Baldy's interest
Was in money business.
        "No interest in any other kind uv bisnis,"
Said Baldy.
        Sleeping with two buck niggers chained to him,
Guardia regia, chained to his waist
To keep 'em from slipping off in the night;
Being by now unpopular with the Cubans;
        By fever reduced to lbs. 108.
Returned to Manhattan, ultimately to Manhattan.
24 E. 47th, when I met him,
Doing job printing, i.e., agent,
        going to his old acquaintances,
His office in Nassau St., distributing jobs to the printers,
Commercial stationery,
        and later, insurance,
Employers' liability,
        odd sorts of insurance,
Fire on brothels, etc., commission,

Rising from 15 dollars a week,
       Pollon d'anthropon iden,
Knew which shipping companies were most careless;
       where a man was most likely
To lose a leg in bad hoisting machinery;
Also fire, as when passing a whore-house,
Arrived, miraculous Hermes, by accident,
Two minutes after the proprietor's *angelos*
Had been sent for him.
Saved his people 11,000 in four months
       on that Cuba job,
But they busted,
Also ran up to 40,000 bones on his own,
  Once, but wanted to "eat up the whole'r Wall St."
And dropped it all three weeks later.
Habitat cum Quade, damn good fellow,
Mons Quade who wore a monocle on a wide sable ribbon.
       (Elsewhere recorded).
Dos Santos, José Maria dos Santos,
Hearing that a grain ship
Was wrecked in the estuary of the Tagus,
Bought it at auction, nemo obstabat,
No one else bidding. "Damn fool!" "Maize
Spoiled with salt water,
No use, can't do anything with it." Dos Santos.
All the stuff rotted with sea water.
Dos Santos Portuguese lunatic bought it,
Mortgaged then all his patrimony,
       e tot lo sieu aver,
And bought sucking pigs, pigs, small pigs,
Porkers, throughout all Portugal,
       fed on the cargo,
First lot mortgaged to buy the second lot, undsoweiter,
Porkers of Portugal,
       fattening with the fulness of time,
And Dos Santos fattened, a great landlord of Portugal
Now gathered to his fathers.
       Did it on water-soaked corn.

(Water probably fresh in that estuary)
Go to hell Apovitch, Chicago aint the whole punkin.
        Jim X...
                in a bankers' meeting,
                bored with their hard luck stories,
Bored with their bloomin' primness
                and the little white rims
They wore around inside the edge of their vests
To make 'em look as if they had on two waistcoats,
Told 'em the Tale of the Honest Sailor.
Bored with their proprieties,
                as they sat, the ranked presbyterians,
Directors, dealers through holding companies,
Deacons in churches, owning slum properties,
Alias usurers in excelsis,
                the quintessential essence of usurers,
The purveyors of employment, whining over their 20 p. c.
                and the hard times,
And the bust-up of Brazilian securities
                (S. A. securities),
And the general uncertainty of all investment
Save investment in new bank buildings,
                productive of bank buildings,
And not likely to ease distribution,
Bored with the way their mouths twitched
                over their cigar-ends,
                Said Jim X... :
There once was a pore honest sailor, a heavy drinker,
A hell of a cuss, a rowster, a boozer, and
The drink finally sent him to hospital,
And they operated, and there was a poor whore in
The woman's ward had a kid, while
They were fixing the sailor, and they brought him the kid
When he came to, and said:
                "Here! this is what we took out of you."

An' he looked at it, an' he got better,
And when he left the hospital, quit the drink,

And when he was well enough
       signed on with another ship
And saved up his pay money,
       and kept on savin' his pay money,
And bought a share in the ship,
       and finally had half shares,
Then a ship
       and in time a whole line of steamers;
And educated the kid,
       and when the kid was in college,
The ole sailor was again taken bad
       and the doctors said he was dying,
And the boy came to the bedside,
       and the old sailor said:
"Boy, I'm sorry I can't hang on a bit longer,
"You're young yet.
       I leave you re-sponsa-bilities.
"Wish I could ha' waited till you were older,
"More fit to take over the bisness..."
       "But, father,
"Don't, don't talk about me, I'm all right,
"It's you, father."
       "That's it, boy, you said it.
"You called me your father, and I ain't.
"I ain't your dad, no,
"I am not your fader but your moder," quod he,
"Your fader was a rich merchant in Stambouli."

KUNG walked
  by the dynastic temple
and into the cedar grove,
   and then out by the lower river,
And with him Khieu, Tchi
   and Tian the low speaking
And "we are unknown," said Kung,
"You will take up charioteering?
   Then you will become known,
"Or perhaps I should take up charioteering, or archery?
"Or the practice of public speaking?"
And Tseu-lou said, "I would put the defences in order,"
And Khieu said, "If I were lord of a province
I would put it in better order than this is."
And Tchi said, "I would prefer a small mountain temple,
"With order in the observances,
   with a suitable performance of the ritual,"
And Tian said, with his hand on the strings of his lute
The low sounds continuing
   after his hand left the strings,
And the sound went up like smoke, under the leaves,
And he looked after the sound:
   "The old swimming hole,
"And the boys flopping off the planks,
"Or sitting in the underbrush playing mandolins."
   And Kung smiled upon all of them equally.
And Thseng-sie desired to know:
   "Which had answered correctly?"
And Kung said, "They have all answered correctly,
"That is to say, each in his nature."
And Kung raised his cane against Yuan Jang,
   Yuan Jang being his elder,
For Yuan Jang sat by the roadside pretending to
   be receiving wisdom.
And Kung said
   "You old fool, come out of it,

Get up and do something useful."
        And Kung said
"Respect a child's faculties
"From the moment it inhales the clear air,
"But a man of fifty who knows nothing
        Is worthy of no respect."
And "When the prince has gathered about him
All the savants and artists, his riches will be fully employed."
And Kung said, and wrote on the bo leaves:
        If a man have not order within him
He can not spread order about him;
And if a man have not order within him
His family will not act with due order;
        And if the prince have not order within him
He can not put order in his dominions.
And Kung gave the words "order"
and "brotherly deference"
And said nothing of the "life after death."
And he said
        "Anyone can run to excesses,
It is easy to shoot past the mark,
It is hard to stand firm in the middle."

And they said: If a man commit murder
        Should his father protect him, and hide him?
And Kung said:
        He should hide him.

And Kung gave his daughter to Kong-Tch'ang
        Although Kong-Tch'ang was in prison.
And he gave his niece to Nan-Young
        although Nan-Young was out of office.
And Kung said "Wang ruled with moderation,
        In his day the State was well kept,
And even I can remember
A day when the historians left blanks in their writings,
I mean for things they didn't know,
But that time seems to be passing."

And Kung said, "Without character you will
          be unable to play on that instrument
Or to execute the music fit for the Odes.
The blossoms of the apricot
          blow from the east to the west,
And I have tried to keep them from falling."

XIV

IO venni in luogo d'ogni luce muto;
The stench of wet coal, politicians
. . . . e and . . . . . n, their wrists bound to their
    ankles,
Standing bare bum,
Faces smeared on their rumps,
        wide eye on flat buttock,
Bush hanging for beard,
    Addressing crowds through their arse-holes,
Addressing the multitudes in the ooze,
        newts, water-slugs, water-maggots,
And with them . . . . r,
        a scrupulously clean table-napkin
Tucked under his penis,
        and . . . . m
Who disliked colloquial language,
Stiff-starched, but soiled, collars
        circumscribing his legs,
The pimply and hairy skin
        pushing over the collar's edge,
Profiteers drinking blood sweetened with sh-t,
And behind them . . . . . . f and the financiers
        lashing them with steel wires.

And the betrayers of language
      . . . . . . n and the press gang
And those who had lied for hire;
the perverts, the perverters of language,
        the perverts, who have set money-lust
Before the pleasures of the senses;

howling, as of a hen-yard in a printing-house,
        the clatter of presses,
the blowing of dry dust and stray paper,
fœtor, sweat, the stench of stale oranges,
dung, last cess-pool of the universe,

mysterium, acid of sulphur,
the pusillanimous, raging;
plunging jewels in mud,
        and howling to find them unstained;
sadic mothers driving their daughters to bed with decrepitude,
sows eating their litters,
and here the placard ΕΙΚΩΝ ΓΗΣ,
        and here: THE PERSONNEL CHANGES,

. melting like dirty wax,
        decayed candles, the bums sinking lower,
faces submerged under hams,
And in the ooze under them,
reversed, foot-palm to foot-palm,
        hand-palm to hand-palm, the agents provocateurs
The murderers of Pearse and MacDonagh,
        Captain H. the chief torturer;
The petrified turd that was Verres,
        bigots, Calvin and St. Clement of Alexandria!
black-beetles, burrowing into the sh-t,
The soil a decrepitude, the ooze full of morsels,
lost contours, erosions.

        Above the hell-rot
the great arse-hole,
        broken with piles,
hanging stalactites,
        greasy as sky over Westminster,
the invisible, many English,
        the place lacking in interest,
last squalor, utter decrepitude,
the vice-crusaders, fahrting through silk,
        waving the Christian symbols,
. . . . frigging a tin penny whistle,
Flies carrying news, harpies dripping sh-t through the air,

The slough of unamiable liars,
        bog of stupidities,

malevolent stupidities, and stupidities,
the soil living pus, full of vermin,
dead maggots begetting live maggots,
      slum owners,
usurers squeezing crab-lice, pandars to authority,
pets-de-loup, sitting on piles of stone books,
obscuring the texts with philology,
      hiding them under their persons,
the air without refuge of silence,
      the drift of lice, teething,
and above it the mouthing of orators,
      the arse-belching of preachers.
      And Invidia,
the corruptio, fœtor, fungus,
liquid animals, melted ossifications,
slow rot, fœtid combustion,
    chewed cigar-butts, without dignity, without tragedy,
. . . . .m Episcopus, waving a condom full of black-beetles,
monopolists, obstructors of knowledge,
      obstructors of distribution.

XV

THE saccharescent, lying in glucose,
the pompous in cotton wool
        with a stench like the fats at Grasse,
the great scabrous arse-hole, sh-tting flies,
        rumbling with imperialism,
ultimate urinal, middan, pisswallow without a cloaca,
. . . . . . r less rowdy, ... Episcopus
        . . . . sis,
        head down, screwed into the swill,
his legs waving and pustular,
        a clerical jock strap hanging back over the navel
his condom full of black beetles,
        tattoo marks round the anus,
and a circle of lady golfers about him.

the courageous violent
        slashing themselves with knives,
the cowardly inciters to violence
. . . . . n and. . . . . . . .h eaten by weevils,
. . . . ll like a swollen fœtus,
        the beast with a hundred legs, USURA
and the swill full of respecters,
        bowing to the lords of the place,
explaining its advantages,
        and the laudatores temporis acti
claiming that the sh-t used to be blacker and richer
and the fabians crying for the petrification of putrefaction,
for a new dung-flow cut in lozenges,
the conservatives chatting,
        distinguished by gaiters of slum-flesh,
and the back-scratchers in a great circle,
        complaining of insufficient attention,
the search without end, counterclaim for the missing scratch
the litigious,
a green bile-sweat, the news owners, ... s
        the anonymous

. . . . ffe, broken
       his head shot like a cannon-ball toward the glass gate,
peering through it an instant,
       falling back to the trunk, epileptic,
et nulla fidentia inter eos,
       all with their twitching backs,
with daggers, and bottle ends, waiting an
       unguarded moment;

a stench, stuck in the nostrils;
beneath one
       nothing that might not move,
mobile earth, a dung hatching obscenities,
       inchoate error,
boredom born out of boredom,
british weeklies, copies of the . . . . c,
a multiple . . . . . . nn,
and I said, "How is it done?"
       and my guide:
This sort breeds by scission,
This is the fourmillionth tumour.
In this *bolge* bores are gathered,
Infinite pus flakes, scabs of a lasting pox.

skin-flakes, repetitions, erosions,
endless rain from the arse-hairs,
as the earth moves, the centre
     passes over all parts in succession,
a continual bum-belch
       distributing its productions.

Andiamo!
      One's feet sunk,
the welsh of mud gripped one, no hand-rail,
the bog-suck like a whirl-pool,
and he said:
       Close the pores of your feet!

And my eyes clung to the horizon,
        oil mixing with soot;
and again Plotinus:
        To the door,
Keep your eyes on the mirror.
Prayed we to the Medusa,
        petrifying the soil by the shield,
Holding it downward
        he hardened the track
Inch before us, by inch,
        the matter resisting,
The heads rose from the shield,
        hissing, held downwards.
Devouring maggots,
        the face only half potent,
The serpents' tongues
        grazing the swill top,
Hammering the souse into hardness,
        the narrow rast,
Half the width of a sword's edge.
        By this through the dern evil,
now sinking, now clinging,
        Holding the unsinkable shield.
Oblivion,
        forget how long,
sleep, fainting nausea.
        "Whether in Naishapur or Babylon"
I heard in the dream.
        Plotinus gone,
And the shield tied under me, woke;
The gate swung on its hinges;
Panting like a sick dog, staggered,
Bathed in alkali, and in acid.
Ἠέλιον τ' Ἠέλιον
        blind with the sunlight,
Swollen-eyed, rested,
        lids sinking, darkness unconscious.

XVI

AND before hell mouth; dry plain
     and two mountains;
On the one mountain, a running form,
     and another
In the turn of the hill; in hard steel
The road like a slow screw's thread,
The angle almost imperceptible,
     so that the circuit seemed hardly to rise;
And the running form, naked, Blake,
Shouting, whirling his arms, the swift limbs,
Howling against the evil,
     his eyes rolling,
Whirling like flaming cart-wheels,
     and his head held backward to gaze on the evil
As he ran from it,
     to be hid by the steel mountain,
And when he showed again from the north side;
     his eyes blazing toward hell mouth,
His neck forward,
     and like him Peire Cardinal.
And in the west mountain, Il Fiorentino,
Seeing hell in his mirror,
     and lo Sordels
Looking on it in his shield;
And Augustine, gazing toward the invisible.

And past them, the criminal
     lying in blue lakes of acid,
The road between the two hills, upward
     slowly,
The flames patterned in lacquer, crimen est actio,
The limbo of chopped ice and saw-dust,
And I bathed myself with the acid to free myself
     of the hell ticks,
Scales, fallen louse eggs.
     Palux Laerna,

the lake of bodies, aqua morta,
of limbs fluid, and mingled, like fish heaped in a bin,
and here an arm upward, clutching a fragment of marble,
And the embryos, in flux,
          new inflow, submerging,
Here an arm upward, trout, submerged by the eels;
          and from the bank, the stiff herbage
the dry nobbled path, saw many known, and unknown,
for an instant;
          submerging,
The face gone, generation.

          Then light air, under saplings,
the blue banded lake under æther,
          an oasis, the stones, the calm field,
the grass quiet,
          and passing the tree of the bough
The grey stone posts,
          and the stair of gray stone,
the passage clean-squared in granite:
          descending,
and I through this, and into the earth,
          patet terra,
entered the quiet air
          the new sky,
the light as after a sun-set,
          and by their fountains, the heroes,
Sigismundo, and Malatesta Novello,
          and founders, gazing at the mounts of their cities.

The plain, distance, and in fount-pools
          the nymphs of that water
rising, spreading their garlands,
          weaving their water reeds with the boughs,
In the quiet,
          and now one man rose from his fountain
and went off into the plain.

Prone in that grass, in sleep;
　　　　et j'entendis des voix:...
　　　　　　　　　　　　　　　wall . . . Strasbourg
Galliffet led that triple charge. . . Prussians
and he said　　　　　　　　　　　　　[*Plarr's narration*]
　　　　it was for the honour of the army.
And they called him a swashbuckler.
　　　　I didn't know what it was
But I thought:　This is pretty bloody damn fine.
And my old nurse, he was a man nurse, and
He killed a Prussian and he lay in the street
there in front of our house for three days
And he stank. . . . . .
　　　　Brother Percy,
And our Brother Percy...
　　　　old Admiral
He was a middy in those days,
And they came into Ragusa
. . . . . . place those men went for the Silk War. . . . .
And they saw a procession coming down through
A cut in the hills, carrying something
The six chaps in front carrying a long thing
　　　　on their shoulders,
And they thought it was a funeral,
　　　　but the thing was wrapped up in scarlet,
And he put off in the cutter,
　　　　he was a middy in those days,
To see what the natives were doing,
And they got up to the six fellows in livery,
And they looked at it, and I can still hear the old admiral,
"Was it? it was
　　　　Lord Byron
Dead drunk, with the face of an A y n. . . . .
He pulled it out long, like that:
　　　　the face of an a y n . . . . gel."

And because that son of a bitch,
　　　　Franz Josef of Austria. . . . . .

: 275 :

And because that son of a bitch Napoléon Barbiche...
They put Aldington on Hill 70, in a trench
        dug through corpses
With a lot of kids of sixteen,
Howling and crying for their mamas,
And he sent a chit back to his major:
        I can hold out for ten minutes
With my sergeant and a machine-gun.
        And they rebuked him for levity.
And Henri Gaudier went to it,
        and they killed him,
And killed a good deal of sculpture,
And ole T.E.H. he went to it,
With a lot of books from the library,
London Library, and a shell buried 'em in a dug-out,
And the Library expressed its annoyance.
        And a bullet hit him on the elbow
...gone through the fellow in front of him,
And he read Kant in the Hospital, in Wimbledon,
in the original,
And the hospital staff didn't like it.

And Wyndham Lewis went to it,
With a heavy bit of artillery,
        and the airmen came by with a mitrailleuse,
And cleaned out most of his company,
        and a shell lit on his tin hut,
While he was out in the privvy,
        and he was all there was left of that outfit.

Windeler went to it,
        and he was out in the Ægæan,
And down in the hold of his ship
        pumping gas into a sausage,
And the boatswain looked over the rail,
        down into amidships, and he said:
        Gees! look a' the Kept'n,
The Kept'n's a-gettin' 'er up.

And Ole Captain Baker went to it,
        with his legs full of rheumatics,
So much so he couldn't run,
        so he was six months in hospital,
Observing the mentality of the patients.

And Fletcher was 19 when he went to it,
And his major went mad in the control pit,
        about midnight, and started throwing the 'phone about
And he had to keep him quiet
        till about six in the morning,
And direct that bunch of artillery.

And Ernie Hemingway went to it,
        too much in a hurry,
And they buried him for four days.

Et ma foi, vous savez,
        tous les nerveux.   Non,
Y a une limite; les bêtes, les bêtes ne sont
Pas faites pour ça, c'est peu de chose un cheval.
Les hommes de 34 ans à quatre pattes
        qui criaient "maman." Mais les costauds,
La fin, là à Verdun, n'y avait que ces gros bonshommes
        Et y voyaient extrêmement clair.
Qu'est-ce que ça vaut, les généraux, le lieutenant,
on les pèse à un centigramme,
        n'y a rien que du bois,
Notr' capitaine, tout, tout ce qu'il y a de plus renfermé
        de vieux polytechnicien, mais solide,
La tête solide.   Là, vous savez,
Tout, tout fonctionne, et les voleurs, tous les vices,
Mais les rapaces,
        y avait trois dans notre compagnie, tous tués.
Y sortaient fouiller un cadavre, pour rien,
        y n'seraient sortis pour rien que ça.
Et les boches, tout ce que vous voulez,
        militarisme, et cætera, et cætera.

Tout ça, mais, MAIS,
        l'français, i s'bat quand y a mangé.
Mais ces pauvres types
A la fin y s'attaquaient pour manger,
        Sans ordres, les bêtes sauvages, on y fait
Prisonniers; ceux qui parlaient français disaient:
        "Poo quah?   Ma foi on attaquait pour manger."

C'est le corr-ggras, le corps gras,
        leurs trains marchaient trois kilomètres à l'heure,
Et ça criait, ça grinçait, on l'entendait à cinq kilomètres.
(Ça qui finit la guerre.)

        Liste officielle des morts 5,000,000.

I vous dit, bè, voui, tout sentait le pétrole.
Mais, Non! je l'ai engueulé.
Je lui ai dit: T'es un con!   T'a raté la guerre.

O voui! tous les hommes de goût, y conviens,
Tout ça en arrière.
        Mais un mec comme toi!
C't homme, un type comme ça!
        Ce qu'il aurait pu encaisser!
Il était dans une fabrique.
What, burying squad, terrassiers, avec leur tête
        en arrière, qui regardaient comme ça,
On risquait la vie pour un coup de pelle,
Faut que ça soit bien carré, exact...

Dey vus a bolcheviki dere, und dey dease him:
Looka vat youah Trotzsk is done, e iss
        madeh deh zhamefull beace!!
"He is iss madeh deh zhamefull beace, iss he?
        "He is madeh de zhamevul beace?
"A Brest-Litovsk, yess?   Aint yuh herd?
        "He vinneh de vore.

"De droobs iss released vrom de eastern vront, yess?
"Un venn dey getts to deh vestern vront, iss it
        "How many getts dere?
"And dose doat getts dere iss so full off revolutions
"Venn deh vrench is come dhru, yess,
"Dey say, "Vot?"   Un de posch say:
        "Aint yeh heard?   Say, ve got a rheffolution."

That's the trick with a crowd,
        Get 'em into the street and get 'em moving.
And all the time, there were people going
Down there, over the river.

        There was a man there talking,
To a thousand, just a short speech, and
Then move 'em on.   And he said:
Yes, these people, they are all right, they
Can do everything, everything except act;
And go an' hear 'em, but when they are through,
Come to the bolsheviki...
And when it broke, there was the crowd there,
And the cossacks, just as always before,
But one thing, the cossacks said:
        "Pojalouista."
And that got round in the crowd,
And then a lieutenant of infantry
Ordered 'em to fire into the crowd,
        in the square at the end of the Nevsky,
In front of the Moscow station,
And they wouldn't,
And he pulled his sword on a student for laughing,
And killed him,
And a cossack rode out of his squad
On the other side of the square
And cut down the lieutenant of infantry
And that was the revolution...
        as soon as they named it.

And you can't make 'em,
Nobody knew it was coming.   They were all ready, the old gang,
Guns on the top of the post-office and the palace,
But none of the leaders knew it was coming.

And there were some killed at the barracks,
But that was between the troops.

So we used to hear it at the opera,
That they wouldn't be under Haig;
          and that the advance was beginning;
That it was going to begin in a week.

XVII

SO that the vines burst from my fingers
And the bees weighted with pollen
Move heavily in the vine-shoots:
       chirr—chirr—chir-rikk—a purring sound,
And the birds sleepily in the branches.
      ZAGREUS! IO ZAGREUS!
With the first pale-clear of the heaven
And the cities set in their hills,
And the goddess of the fair knees
Moving there, with the oak-woods behind her,
The green slope, with white hounds
        leaping about her;
And thence down to the creek's mouth, until evening,
Flat water before me,
      and the trees growing in water,
Marble trunks out of stillness,
On past the palazzi,
         in the stillness,
The light now, not of the sun.
         Chrysophrase,
And the water green clear, and blue clear;
On, to the great cliffs of amber.
            Between them,
Cave of Nerea,
   she like a great shell curved,
And the boat drawn without sound,
Without odour of ship-work,
Nor bird-cry, nor any noise of wave moving,
Nor splash of porpoise, nor any noise of wave moving,
Within her cave, Nerea,
         she like a great shell curved
In the suavity of the rock,
        cliff green-gray in the far,
In the near, the gate-cliffs of amber,
And the wave
      green clear, and blue clear,

And the cave salt-white, and glare-purple,
            cool, porphyry smooth,
            the rock sea-worn.
No gull-cry, no sound of porpoise,
Sand as of malachite, and no cold there,
            the light not of the sun.

Zagreus, feeding his panthers,
            the turf clear as on hills under light.
And under the almond-trees, gods,
            with them, *choros nympharum*.   Gods,
Hermes and Athene,
                        As shaft of compass,
Between them, trembled—
To the left is the place of fauns,
                        sylva nympharum;
The low wood, moor-scrub,
            the doe, the young spotted deer,
            leap up through the broom-plants,
                        as dry leaf amid yellow.
And by one cut of the hills,
            the great alley of Memnons.
Beyond, sea, crests seen over dune
Night sea churning shingle,
To the left, the alley of cypress.
                        A boat came,
One man holding her sail,
Guiding her with oar caught over gunwale, saying:
"   There, in the forest of marble,
"   the stone trees—out of water—
"   the arbours of stone—
"   marble leaf, over leaf,
"   silver, steel over steel,
"   silver beaks rising and crossing,
"   prow set against prow,
"   stone, ply over ply,
"   the gilt beams flare of an evening"
Borso, Carmagnola, the men of craft, *i vitrei*,

Thither, at one time, time after time,
And the waters richer than glass,
Bronze gold, the blaze over the silver,
Dye-pots in the torch-light,
The flash of wave under prows,
And the silver beaks rising and crossing.
                Stone trees, white and rose-white in the darkness,
Cypress there by the towers,
                Drift under hulls in the night.

                "In the gloom the gold
Gathers the light about it."...

Now supine in burrow, half over-arched bramble,
One eye for the sea, through that peek-hole,
Gray light, with Athene.
Zothar and her elephants, the gold loin-cloth,
The sistrum, shaken, shaken,
                the cohorts of her dancers.
And Aletha, by bend of the shore,
                with her eyes seaward,
                and in her hands sea-wrack
Salt-bright with the foam.
Koré through the bright meadow,
                with green-gray dust in the grass:
"For this hour, brother of Circe."
Arm laid over my shoulder,
Saw the sun for three days, the sun fulvid,
As a lion lift over sand-plain;
                                and that day,
And for three days, and none after,
Splendour, as the splendour of Hermes,
And shipped thence
                to the stone place,
Pale white, over water,
                known water,
And the white forest of marble, bent bough over bough,
The pleached arbour of stone,

Thither Borso, when they shot the barbed arrow at him,
And Carmagnola, between the two columns,
Sigismundo, after that wreck in Dalmatia.
    Sunset like the grasshopper flying.

XVIII

AND of Kublai:
"I have told you of that emperor's city in detail
And will tell you of the coining in Cambaluc
          that hyght the secret of alchemy:
They take bast of the mulberry-tree,
That is a skin between the wood and the bark,
And of this they make paper, and mark it
Half a tornesel, a tornesel, or a half-groat of silver,
Or two groats, or five groats, or ten groats,
Or, for a great sheet, a gold bezant, 3 bezants,
          ten bezants;
And they are written on by officials,
And smeared with the great khan's seal in vermilion;
And the forgers are punished with death.
And all this costs the Kahn nothing,
And so he is rich in this world.
And his postmen go sewed up and sealed up,
Their coats buttoned behind and then sealed,
In this way from the voyage's one end to its other.
And the Indian merchants arriving
Must give up their jewels, and take this money
          in paper,
(That trade runs, in bezants, to 400,000 the year.)
And the nobles must buy their pearls"
—thus Messire Polo; prison at Genoa—
"Of the Emperor."
          There was a boy in Constantinople,
And some britisher kicked his arse.
"I hate these french," said Napoleon, aged 12,
To young Bourrienne, "I will do them all the harm that I can."
In like manner Zenos Metevsky.
And old Biers was out there, a greenhorn,
To sell cannon, and Metevsky found the back door;
And old Biers sold the munitions,
And Metevsky died and was buried, *i. e.* officially,
And sat in the Yeiner Kafé watching the funeral.

About ten years after this incident,
He owned a fair chunk of Humbers.
                    "Peace!   Pieyce!!" said Mr. Giddings,
"Uni-ver-sal?   Not while yew got tew billions ov money,"
Said Mr. Giddings, "invested in the man-u-facture
"Of war machinery.   Haow I sold it to Russia—
"Well we tuk 'em a new torpedo-boat,
"And it was all electric, run it all from a
"Little bit uv a keyboard, about like the size ov
"A typewriter, and the prince come aboard,
"An' we sez wud yew like to run her?
"And he run damn slam on the breakwater,
"And bust off all her front end,
"And he was my gawd scared out of his panties.
"Who wuz agoin' tew pay fer the damage?
"And it was my first trip out fer the company,
"And I sez, yer highness, it is nothing,
"We will give yew a new one.   And, my Christ!
"The company backed me, and did we get a few orders?"
So La Marquesa de las Zojas y Hurbara
Used to drive up to Sir Zenos's placc
                    in the Champs Elysées
And preside at his dinners, and at *las once*
She drove away from the front door, with her footmen
And her coachman in livery, and drove four blocks round
To the back door, and her husband was the son of a bitch,
And Metevsky, "the well-known philanthropist,"
Or "the well-known financier, better known,"
As the press said, "as a philanthropist,"
Gave—as the Este to Louis Eleventh,—
A fine pair of giraffes to the nation,
And endowed a chair of ballistics,
And was consulted before the offensives.

And Mr. Oige was very choleric in a first-class
From Nice to Paris, he said: "Danger!
"Now a sailor's life is a life of danger,
"But a mine, why every stick of it is numbered,

"And one time we missed one, and there was
"Three hundred men killed in the 'splosion."
He was annoyed with the strikers, having started himself
As engineer and worked up, and losing,
By that coal strike, some months after the paragraph:

:Sir Zenos Metevsky has been elected President
Of the Gethsemane Trebizond Petrol.
And then there came out another: 80 locomotives
On the Manchester Cardiff have been fitted with
New oil-burning apparatus...
Large stocks of the heavier varieties of which (*i. e.* oil)
Are now on hand in the country.

So I said to the old quaker Hamish,
I said: "I am interested."   And he went putty colour
And said: "He don't advertise.   No, I don't think
You will learn much."   That was when I asked
About Metevsky Melchizedek.
He, Hamish, took the tractors up to
King Menelik, 3 rivers and 140 ravines.

"Qu'est-ce qu'on pense...?"   I said: "On don't pense.
"They're solid bone.   You can amputate from just above
The medulla, and it won't alter the life in that island."
But he continued, "Mais, qu'EST-CE qu'ON pense,
"De la metallurgie, en Angleterre, qu'est-ce qu'on
"Pense de Metevsky?"
And I said: "They ain't heard his name yet.
"Go ask at MacGorvish's bank."

The Jap observers were much amused because
The Turkish freemasons hadn't bothered to
Take the..... regimental badges off their artillery.
And old Hamish: Menelik
Had a hunch that machinery...and so on...
But he never could get it to work,
            never could get any power.

The Germans wd. send him up boilers, but they'd
Have to cut 'em into pieces to load 'em on camels,
And they never got 'em together again.
And so old Hamish went out there,
And looked at the place, 3 rivers
And a hundred and forty ravines,
And he sent out two tractors, one to pull on the other
And Menelik sent down an army, a 5000 black army
With hawsers, and they all sweated and swatted.

And the first thing Dave lit on when they got there
Was a buzz-saw,
And he put it through an ebony log: whhsssh, t ttt,
Two days' work in three minutes.

War, one war after another,
Men start 'em who couldn't put up a good hen-roost.

Also sabotage...

XIX

SABOTAGE?   Yes, he took it up to Manhattan,
To the big company, and they said: Impossible.
And he said: I gawt ten thousand dollars tew mak 'em,
And I am a goin' tew mak 'em, and you'll damn well
Have to install 'em, awl over the place.
And they said: Oh, we can't have it.
So he settled for one-half of one million.
And he has a very nice place on the Hudson,
And that invention, patent, is still in their desk.
And the answer to that is: Wa'al he had the ten thousand.
And old Spinder, that put up the 1870 gothick memorial,
He tried to pull me on Marx, and he told me
About the "romance of his business":
How he came to England with something or other,
                            and sold it.
Only he wanted to talk about Marx, so I sez:
Waal haow is it you're over here, right off the
                            Champz Elyza?
And how can yew be here?   Why don't the fellers at home
Take it all off you?   How can you leave your big business?
"Oh," he sez, "I ain't had to rent any money...
"It's a long time since I ain't had tew rent any money."
Nawthin' more about Das Kapital,
Or credit, or distribution.
And he "never finished the book,"
That was the other chap, the slender diplomatdentist
Qui se faisait si beau.

So we sat there, with the old kindly professor,
And the stubby little man was up-stairs.
And there was the slick guy in the other
corner reading The Tatler,
Not upside down, but never turning the pages,
And then I went up to the bed-room, and he said,
The stubby fellow: Perfectly true,
"But it's a question of feeling,

"Can't move 'em with a cold thing, like economics."
And so we came down stairs and went out,
And the slick guy looked out of the window,
And in came the street "Lemme-at-'em"
                        like a bull-dog in a mackintosh.
                        O my Clio!
Then the telephone didn't work for a week.

Ever seen Prishnip, little hunchback,
Couldn't take him for *any* army.
And he said: I haf a messache from dh' professor,
"There's lots of 'em want to go over,
"But when they try to go over,
"Dh' hRussian boys shoot 'em, and they want to know
"How to go over."

Vlettmann?...was out there, and that was,
Say, two months later, and he said:
"Jolly chaps," he said; "they used to go by
"Under my window, at two o'clock in the morning,
"All singing, all singing the *Hé Sloveny!*"

Yes, Vlettmann, and the Russian boys didn't shoot'em.
      Short story, entitled, the Birth of a Nation.
And there was that squirt of an Ausstrrian
              with a rose in his button-hole,
And how the hell he stayed on here,
              right through the whole bhloody business,
Cocky as Khristnoze, and enjoying every Boche victory.
Naphtha, or some damn thing for the submarines,
Like they had, just *had*, to have the hemp
              via Rotterdam.
Das thust du nicht, Albert?
That was in the old days, all sitting around in arm-chairs,
And that's gone, like the cake shops in the Nevsky.
"No use telling 'em anything, revolutionaries,
Till they're at the *end*,

Oh, absolootly, AT the end of their tether.
Governed. Governed the place from a train,
Or rather from three trains, on a railway,
And he'd keep about three days ahead of the lobby,
I mean he had his government on the trains,
And the lobby had to get there on horseback;
And he said: Bigod it's damn funny,
Own half the oil in the world, and can't get enough
To run a government engine!"
And then they jawed for two hours,
And finally Steff said: Will you fellows show me a map?
And they brought one, and Steff said:
"Waal what are those lines?" "Yes, those straight lines."
"Those are roads." And "what are those lines,
"The wiggly ones?" "Rivers."
And Steff said: "Government property?"

So two hours later an engine went off with the order:
How to dig without confiscation.

And Tommy Baymont said to Steff one day:
"You think we run it, lemme tell you,
"We bought a coalmine, I mean the mortgage fell in,
"And you'd a' thought we could run it.

"Well I had to go down there meself, and the manager
"Said: "Run it, of course we can run it,
"We can't sell the damn coal."

So I said to the X. and B. Central,
—you'd say we boss the X. and B. Central?—
I said: You buy your damn coal from our mine.
And a year later they hadn't; so I had up the directors,
And they said:...well anyhow, they couldn't
                    buy the damn coal.
And next week ole Jim came, the big fat one
With the diamonds, and he said: "Mr. Baymont,

You just *must* charge two dollars more
A ton fer that coal.   And the X. and B. will
Take it through us."

"So there was my ole man sitting,
They were in arm-chairs, according to protocol,
And next him his nephew Mr. Wurmsdorf,
And old Ptierstoff, for purely family reasons,
Personal reasons, was held in great esteem
                    by his relatives,
And he had his despatches from St. Petersburg,
And Wurmsdorf had his from Vienna,
And he knew and they knew, and each knew
That the other knew that the other knew he knew,
And Wurmsdorf was just reaching into his pocket,
That was to start things, and then my ole man
Said it:
          Albert, and the rest of it.
Those days are gone by for ever."

"Ten years gone, ten years of my life,
Never get those ten years back again:
Ten years of my life, ten years in the Indian army;
But anyhow, there was that time in Yash (Jassy):
That was something, 14 girls in a fortnight."
"Healthy but verminous?"   "That's it, healthy but verminous.
                    And one time in Kashmir,
In the houseboats, with the turquoise,
A pile three feet high on the boat floor,
And they'd be there all day at a bargain
For ten bobs' worth of turquoise."

XX

"SOUND slender, quasi tinnula,
Ligur' aoide: Si no'us vei, Domna don plus mi cal,
Negus vezer mon bel pensar no val."
Between the two almond trees flowering,
The viel held close to his side;
And another: "s'adora."
"Possum ego naturae
non meminisse tuae!" Qui son Properzio ed Ovidio.

The boughs are not more fresh
where the almond shoots
take their March green.
And that year I went up to Freiburg,
And Rennert had said: Nobody, no, nobody
Knows anything about Provençal, or if there is anybody,
It's old Lévy."
And so I went up to Freiburg,
And the vacation was just beginning,
The students getting off for the summer,
Freiburg im Breisgau,
And everything clean, seeming clean, after Italy.

And I went to old Lévy, and it was by then 6.30
in the evening, and he trailed half way across Freiburg
before dinner, to see the two strips of copy,
Arnaut's, settant'uno R. superiore (Ambrosiana)
Not that I could sing him the music.
And he said: Now is there anything I can tell you?"
And I said: I dunno, sir, or
"Yes, Doctor, what do they mean by *noigandres?*"
And he said: Noigandres! NOIgandres!
"You know for seex mon's of my life
"Effery night when I go to bett, I say to myself:
"Noigandres, eh, *noigandres,*
"Now what the DEFFIL can that mean!"
Wind over the olive trees, ranunculæ ordered,

By the clear edge of the rocks
The water runs, and the wind scented with pine
And with hay-fields under sun-swath.
Agostino, Jacopo and Boccata
You would be happy for the smell of that place
And never tired of being there, either alone
Or accompanied.
Sound: as of the nightingale too far off to be heard.
Sandro, and Boccata, and Jacopo Sellaio;
The ranunculæ, and almond,
Boughs set in espalier,
Duccio, Agostino; *e l'olors*—
The smell of that place—*d'enoi ganres*.
Air moving under the boughs,
The cedars there in the sun,
Hay new cut on hill slope,
And the water there in the cut
Between the two lower meadows; sound,
The sound, as I have said, a nightingale
Too far off to be heard.
And the light falls, *remir*,
from her breast to thighs.

He was playing there at the palla.
Parisina—two doves for an altar—at the window,
"E'l Marchese
Stava per divenir pazzo
after it all."   And that was when Troy was down
And they came here and cut holes in rock,
Down Rome way, and put up the timbers;
And came here, condit Atesten...
          "Peace! keep the peace, Borso."
And he said: Some bitch has sold us
              (that was Ganelon)
"They wont get another such ivory."
And he lay there on the round hill under the cedar
A little to the left of the cut (Este speaking)

By the side of the summit, and he said:
            "I have broken the horn, bigod, I have
"Broke the best ivory, l'olofans."   And he said:
"Tan mare fustes!"
                pulling himself over the gravel,
"Bigod! that buggar is done for,
"They wont get another such ivory."
And they were there before the wall, Toro, las almenas,
(Este, Nic Este speaking)
                        Under the battlement
(Epi purgo) peur de la hasle,
And the King said:
                "God what a woman!
My God what a woman" said the King telo rigido.
"Sister!" says Ancures, "'s your sister!"
Alf left that town to Elvira, and Sancho wanted
It from her, Toro and Zamora.
                        "Bloody spaniard!
Neestho, le'er go back...
                    in the autumn."
"Este, go' damn you." between the walls, arras,
Painted to look like arras.
                    Jungle:
Glaze green and red feathers, jungle,
Basis of renewal, renewals;
Rising over the soul, green virid, of the jungle,
Lozenge of the pavement, clear shapes,
Broken, disrupted, body eternal,
Wilderness of renewals, confusion
Basis of renewals, subsistence,
Glazed green of the jungle;
Zoe, Marozia, Zothar,
                    loud over the banners,
Glazed grape, and the crimson,
HO BIOS,
            cosi Elena vedi,
In the sunlight, gate cut by the shadow;

And then the faceted air:
Floating.　Below, sea churning shingle.
Floating, each on invisible raft,
On the high current, invisible fluid,
Borne over the plain, recumbent,
The right arm cast back,
　　　　the right wrist for a pillow,
The left hand like a calyx,
Thumb held against finger, the third,
The first fingers petal'd up, the hand as a lamp,
A calyx.
　　　　From toe to head
The purple, blue-pale smoke, as of incense;
Wrapped each in burnous, smoke as the olibanum's,
Swift, as if joyous.
Wrapped, floating; and the blue-pale smoke of the incense
Swift to rise, then lazily in the wind
　　　　as Aeolus over bean-field,
As hay in the sun, the olibanum, saffron,
As myrrh without styrax;
Each man in his cloth, as on raft, on
　　　　The high invisible current;
On toward the fall of water;
And then over that cataract,
In air, strong, the bright flames, V shaped;
　　　　Nel fuoco
D'amore mi mise, nel fuoco d'amore mi mise...
Yellow, bright saffron, croceo;
And as the olibanum bursts into flame,
The bodies so flamed in the air, took flame,
　　　　"...Mi mise, il mio sposo novello."
Shot from stream into spiral,

Or followed the water.　Or looked back to the flowing;
Others approaching that cataract,
As to dawn out of shadow, the swathed cloths
Now purple and orange,

And the blue water dusky beneath them,
        pouring there into the cataract,
With noise of sea over shingle,
           striking with:
           hah hah ahah thmm, thunb, ah
           woh woh araha thumm, bhaaa.
And from the floating bodies, the incense
    blue-pale, purple above them.
Shelf of the lotophagoi,
Aerial, cut in the aether.
               Reclining,
With the silver spilla,
The ball as of melted amber, coiled, caught up, and turned.
Lotophagoi of the suave nails, quiet, scornful,
Voce-profondo:
        "Feared neither death nor pain for this beauty;
If harm, harm to ourselves."
And beneath: the clear bones, far down,
Thousand on thousand.
        "What gain with Odysseus,
"They that died in the whirlpool
"And after many vain labours,
"Living by stolen meat, chained to the rowingbench,
"That he should have a great fame
        "And lie by night with the goddess?
"Their names are not written in bronze
        "Nor their rowing sticks set with Elpenor's;
"Nor have they mound by sea-bord.
        "That saw never the olives under Spartha
"With the leaves green and then not green,
        "The click of light in their branches;
"That saw not the bronze hall nor the ingle
"Nor lay there with the queen's waiting maids,
"Nor had they Circe to couch-mate, Circe Titania,
"Nor had they meats of Kalüpso
"Or her silk skirts brushing their thighs.
"Give!   What were they given?

Ear-wax.

"Poison and ear-wax,
                    and a salt grave by the bull-field,
"neson amumona, their heads like sea crows in the foam,
"Black splotches, sea-weed under lightning;
"Canned beef of Apollo, ten cans for a boat load."
Ligur' aoide.

And from the plain whence the water-shoot,
Across, back, to the right, the roads, a way in the grass,
The Khan's hunting leopard, and young Salustio
And Ixotta; the suave turf
Ac ferae familiares, and the cars slowly,
And the panthers, soft-footed.
Plain, as the plain of Somnus,
                    the heavy cars, as a triumph,
Gilded, heavy on wheel,
                    and the panthers chained to the cars,
Over suave turf, the form wrapped,
Rose, crimson, deep crimson,
And, in the blue dusk, a colour as of rust in the sunlight,
Out of white cloud, moving over the plain,
Head in arm's curve, reclining;
The road, back and away, till cut along the face of the rock,
And the cliff folds in like a curtain,
The road cut in under the rock
Square groove in the cliff's face, as chiostri,
The columns crystal, with peacocks cut in the capitals,
The soft pad of beasts dragging the cars;
Cars, slow, without creak,
And at windows in inner roadside:
                    le donne e i cavalieri
                    smooth face under hennin,
The sleeves embroidered with flowers,
Great thistle of gold, or an amaranth,
Acorns of gold, or of scarlet,
Cramoisi and diaspre
                    slashed white into velvet;

Crystal columns, acanthus, sirens in the pillar heads;
And at last, between gilded barocco,
Two columns coiled and fluted,
Vanoka, leaning half naked,
            waste hall there behind her.
"Peace!
            Borso..., Borso!"

XXI

"KEEP the peace, Borso!" Where are we?
"Keep on with the business,
                    That's made me,
"And the res publica didn't.
"When I was broke, and a poor kid,
"They all knew me, all of these *cittadini*,
"And they all of them cut me dead, della gloria."
Intestate, 1429, leaving 178,221 florins *di sugello*,
As is said in Cosimo's red leather note book. Di sugello.
And "with his credit emptied Venice of money"—
That was Cosimo—
"And Naples, and made them accept his peace."
And he caught the young boy Ficino
And had him taught the greek language;
"With two ells of red cloth per person
I will make you," Cosimo speaking, "as many
Honest citizens as you desire."
Col credito suo...
Napoli e Venezia di danari...
Costretti... Napoli e Venezia... a quella pace...
Or another time... oh well, pass it.
And Piero called in the credits,
(Diotisalvi was back of that)
And firms failed as far off as Avignon,
And Piero was like to be murdered,
And young Lauro came down ahead of him, in the road,
And said: Yes, father is coming.

Intestate, '69, in December, leaving me 237,989 florins,
As you will find in my big green account book
In carta di capretto;
And from '34 when I count it, to last year,
We paid out 600,000 and over,
That was for building, taxes and charity.
Nic Uzano saw us coming. Against it, honest,
And warned 'em. They'd have murdered him,

And would Cosimo, but he bribed 'em;
And they did in Giuliano.   E difficile,
A Firenze difficile viver ricco
Senza aver lo stato.
"E non avendo stato Piccinino
"Doveva temerlo qualunque era in stato;"
And "that man sweated blood to put through that railway";
"Could you," wrote Mr. Jefferson,
"Find me a gardener
Who can play the french horn?
The bounds of American fortune
Will not admit the indulgence of a domestic band of
Musicians, yet I have thought that a passion for music
Might be reconciled with that economy which we are
Obliged to observe.   I retain among my domestic servants
A gardener, a weaver, a cabinet-maker, and a stone-cutter,
To which I would add a vigneron.   In a country like yours
(id est Burgundy) where music is cultivated and
Practised by every class of men, I suppose there might
Be found persons of these trades who could perform on
The french horn, clarionet, or hautboy and bassoon, so
That one might have a band of two french horns, two
Clarionets, two hautboys and a bassoon, without enlarging
Their domestic expenses.   A certainty of employment for
Half a dozen years
           (affatigandose per suo piacer o non)
And at the end of that time, to find them, if they
Choose, a conveyance to their own country, might induce
Them to come here on reasonable wages.   Without meaning to
Give you trouble, perhaps it might be practicable for you
In your ordinary intercourse with your people to find out
Such men disposed to come to America.   Sobriety and good
Nature would be desirable parts of their characters"
                                        June 1778 Montecello

And in July I went up to Milan for Duke Galeaz
To sponsor his infant in baptism,
Albeit were others more worthy,

And took his wife a gold collar holding a diamond
That cost about 3000 ducats, on which account
That signor Galeaz Sforza Visconti has wished me
To stand sponsor to all of his children.

Another war without glory, and another peace without quiet.

And the Sultan sent him an assassin, his brother;
And the Soldan of Egypt, a lion;
And he begat one pope and one son and four daughters,
And an University, Pisa; (Lauro Medici)
And nearly went broke in his business,
And bought land in Siena and Pisa,
And made peace by his own talk in Naples.
And there was grass on the floor of the temple,
Or where the floor of it might have been;
      Gold fades in the gloom,
      Under the blue-black roof, Placidia's,
Of the exarchate; and we sit here
By the arena, *les gradins*...
And the palazzo, baseless, hangs there in the dawn
With low mist over the tide-mark;
And floats there nel tramonto
With gold mist over the tide-mark.
The tesserae of the floor, and the patterns.
Fools making new shambles;
        night over green ocean,
And the dry black of the night.
        Night of the golden tiger,
And the dry flame in the air,
        Voices of the procession,
Faint now, from below us,
And the sea with tin flash in the sun-dazzle,
        Like dark wine in the shadows.
"Wind between the sea and the mountains"
 The tree-spheres half dark against sea
        half clear against sunset,

The sun's keel freighted with cloud,
And after that hour, dry darkness
Floating flame in the air, gonads in organdy,
Dry flamelet, a petal borne in the wind.
Gignetei kalon.
Impenetrable as the ignorance of old women.
In the dawn, as the fleet coming in after Actium,
Shore to the eastward, and altered,
And the old man sweeping leaves:
          "Damned to you Midas, Midas lacking a Pan!"
And now in the valley,
Valley under the day's edge:
          "Grow with the Pines of Ise;
"As the Nile swells with Inopos.
          "As the Nile falls with Inopos."
Phoibos, turris eburnea,
          ivory against cobalt,
And the boughs cut on the air,
The leaves cut on the air,
The hounds on the green slope by the hill,
          water still black in the shadow.
In the crisp air,
          the discontinuous gods;
Pallas, young owl in the cup of her hand,
And, by night, the stag runs, and the leopard,
Owl-eye amid pine boughs.
Moon on the palm-leaf,
                    confusion;
Confusion, source of renewals;
Yellow wing, pale in the moon shaft,
Green wing, pale in the moon shaft,
Pomegranate, pale in the moon shaft,
White horn, pale in the moon shaft, and Titania
By the drinking hole,
          steps, cut in the basalt.
Danced there Athame, danced, and there Phæthusa
With colour in the vein,

Strong as with blood-drink, once,
With colour in the vein,
Red in the smoke-faint throat.   Dis caught her up.

And the old man went on there
            beating his mule with an asphodel.

XXII

"AN' that man sweat blood
to put through that railway,
And what he ever got out of it?
And he said one thing: As it costs,
As in any indian war it costs the government
20,000 dollars per head
To kill off the red warriors, it might be more humane
And even cheaper, to educate.
And there was the other type, Warenhauser,
That beat him, and broke up his business,
Tale of the American Curia that gave him,
Warenhauser permission to build the Northwestern railway
And to take the timber he cut in the process;
So he cut a road through the forest,
Two miles wide, an' perfectly legal.
Who wuz agoin' to stop him!

And he came in and said: Can't do it,
Not at that price, we can't do it."
That was in the last war, here in England,
And he was making chunks for a turbine
In some sort of an army plane;
An' the inspector says: "How many rejects?"
"What you mean, rejects?"
And the inspector says: "How many do you get?"
And Joe said: "We don't get *any* rejects, our..."
And the inspector says: "Well then of course
                                you can't do it."
Price of life in the occident.
And C. H. said to the renowned Mr. Bukos:
"What is the cause of the H. C. L.?" and Mr. Bukos,
The economist consulted of nations, said:
                                "Lack of labour."
And there were two millions of men out of work.
And C. H. shut up, he said
He would save his breath to cool his own porridge,

But I didn't, and I went on plaguing Mr. Bukos
Who said finally: "I am an orthodox
"Economist."
                    Jesu Christo!
Standu nel paradiso terrestre
Pensando come si fesse compagna d'Adamo!!

And Mr. H. B. wrote in to the office:
I would like to accept C. H.'s book
But it would make my own seem so out of date.
                    Heaven will protect
The lay reader.   The whole fortune of
Mac Narpen and Company is founded
Upon Palgrave's Golden Treasury.   Nel paradiso terrestre

And all the material was used up, Jesu Christo,
And everything in its place, and nothing left over
To make una compagna d'Adamo.   Come si fesse?
E poi ha vishtu una volpe
And the tail of the volpe, the vixen,
Fine, spreading and handsome, e pensava:
That will do for this business;
And la volpe saw in his eye what was coming,
Corre, volpe corre, Christu corre, volpecorre,
Christucorre, e dav' un saltu, ed ha preso la coda
Della volpe, and the volpe wrenched loose
And left the tail in his hand, e di questu
Fu fatta,
                    e per questu
E la donna una furia,
Una fuRRia-e-una rabbia.
And a voice behind me in the street.
"Meestair Freer!   Meestair..."
And I thought I was three thousand
Miles from the nearest connection;
And he'd known me for three days, years before that,
And he said, one day a week later: Woud you lak
To meet a wholley man, yais he is a veree wholley man.

So I met Mohamed Ben Abt el Hjameed,
And that evening he spent his whole time
Queering the shirt-seller's business,
And taking hot whiskey.   The sailors
Come in there for two nights a week and fill up the café
And the rock scorpions cling to the edge
Until they can't jes' nacherly stand it
And then they go to the Calpe (Lyceo)

NO MEMBER OF THE MILITARY
OF WHATEVER RANK
IS PERMITTED WITHIN THE WALLS
OF THIS CLUB

That fer the governor of Gibel Tara.
"Jeen-jah!   Jeen-jah!" squawked Mohamed,
"O-ah, geef heem sax-pence."
And a chap in a red fez came in, and grinned at Mohamed
Who spat across four metres of tables
At Mustafa.   That was all there was
To that greeting; and three nights later
Ginger came back as a customer, and took it out of Mohamed.
He hadn't sold a damn shirt on the Tuesday.
And I met Yusuf and eight men in the calle,
So I sez: Wot is the matter?
And Yusuf said: Vairy foolish, it will
Be sefen an' seex for the summons
—Mohamed want to sue heem for libel—
To give all that to the court!
        So I went off to Granada
And when I came back I saw Ginger, and I said:
What about it?
        And he said: O-ah, I geef heem a
Seex-pence.   Customs of the sha-ha-reef.
And they were all there in the lyceo,
Cab drivers, and chaps from tobacco shops,

And Edward the Seventh's guide, and they were all
For secession.
Dance halls being closed at two in the morning,
By the governor's order.   And another day on the pier
Was a fat fellah from Rhode Island, a-sayin':
"Bi Hek!   I been all thru Italy
            An' ain't never been stuck!"
"But this place is plumb full er scoundrels."
And Yusuf said: Yais? an' the reech man
In youah countree, haowa they get their money;
They no go rob some poor pairsons?
And the fat fellah shut up, and went off.
And Yusuf said: Woat, he iss all thru Eetaly
An' ee is nevair been stuck, ee ees a liar.
W'en I goa to some forain's country
I am stuck.
            W'en yeou goa to some forain's country
You moss be stuck; w'en they come 'ere I steek thaim.
And we went down to the synagogue,
All full of silver lamps
And the top gallery stacked with old benches;
And in came the levite and six little choir kids
And began yowling the ritual
As if it was crammed full of jokes,
And they went through a whole book of it;
And in came the elders and the scribes
About five or six and the rabbi
And he sat down, and grinned, and pulled out his snuff-box,
And sniffed up a thumb-full, and grinned,
And called over a kid from the choir, and whispered,
And nodded toward one old buffer,
And the kid took him the snuff-box and he grinned,
And bowed his head, and sniffed up a thumb-full,
And the kid took the box back to the rabbi,
And he grinned, e faceva bisbiglio,
And the kid toted off the box to
            another old bunch of whiskers,
And he sniffed up his thumb-full,

And so on till they'd each had his sniff;
And then the rabbi looked at the stranger, and they
All grinned half a yard wider, and the rabbi
Whispered for about two minutes longer,
An' the kid brought the box over to me,
And I grinned and sniffed up my thumb-full.
And then they got out the scrolls of the law
And had their little procession
And kissed the ends of the markers.
And there was a case on for rape and blackmail
Down at the court-house, behind the big patio
          full of wistaria;
An' the nigger in the red fez, Mustafa, on the boat later
An' I said to him: Yusuf, Yusuf's a damn good feller.
And he says:
          "Yais, he ees a goot fello,
"But after all a chew
                    ees a chew."
And the judge says: That veil is too long.
And the girl takes off the veil
That she has stuck onto her hat with a pin,
"Not a veil," she says, "'at's a scarf."
And the judge says:
          Don't you know you aren't allowed all those buttons?
And she says: Those ain't buttons, them's bobbles.
Can't you see there ain't any button-holes?
And the Judge says: Well, anyway, you're not allowed ermine.
"Ermine?" the girl says, "Not ermine, that ain't,
"'At's lattittzo."
And the judge says: And just what is a lattittzo?
And the girl says:
          "It'z a animal."

Signori, *you* go and enforce it.

XXIII

"ET omniformis," Psellos, "omnis
"Intellectus est."   God's fire.   Gemisto:
"Never with this religion
"Will you make men of the greeks.
"But build wall across Peloponesus
"And organize, and...
                damn these Eyetalian barbarians."
And Novvy's ship went down in the tempest
Or at least they chucked the books overboard.

How dissolve Irol in sugar... Houille blanche,
Auto-chenille, destroy all bacteria in the kidney,
Invention-d'entités-plus-ou-moins-abstraits-
en-nombre-égal-aux-choses-à-expliquer...
   La Science ne peut pas y consister.   "J'ai
Obtenu une brulure" M. Curie, or some other scientist
"Qui m'a coûté six mois de guérison."
        and continued his experiments.
Tropismes!   "We believe the attraction is chemical."

With the sun in a golden cup
    and going toward the low fords of ocean
Ἅλιος δ' Ὑπεριονίδας δέπας ἐσκατέβαινε χρύσεον
Ὄφρα δι ὠκεανοῖο περάσας
        ima vada noctis obscurae
Seeking doubtless the sex in bread-moulds
ἥλιος, ἅλιος, ἅλιος = μάταιος
("Derivation uncertain."   The idiot
Odysseus furrowed the sand.)
alixantos, aliotrephès, eiskatebaine, down into,
descended, to the end that, beyond ocean,
pass through, traverse
              ποτὶ βένθεα
νυκτὸς ἐρεμνᾶς,
ποτὶ ματέρα, κουριδίαν τ'ἄλοχον

παῖδάς τε φίλους . . . . ἔβα δάφναισι κατάσκιον
Precisely, the selv' oscura
And in the morning, in the Phrygian head-sack
Barefooted, dumping sand from their boat
'Yperionides!
             And the rose grown while I slept,
And the strings shaken with music,
Capriped, the loose twigs under foot;
We here on the hill, with the olives
Where a man might carry his oar up,
And the boat there in the inlet;
As we had lain there in the autumn
Under the arras, or wall painted below like arras,
And above with a garden of rose-trees,
Sound coming up from the cross-street;
As we had stood there,
Watching road from the window,
Fa Han and I at the window,
And her head bound with gold cords.
Cloud over mountain; hill-gap, in mist, like a sea-coast.

Leaf over leaf, dawn-branch in the sky
And the sea dark, under wind,
The boat's sails hung loose at the mooring,
             Cloud like a sail inverted,
And the men dumping sand by the sea-wall
Olive trees there on the hill
      where a man might carry his oar up.

And my brother De Mænsac
Bet with me for the castle,
And we put it on the toss of a coin,
And I, Austors, won the coin-toss and kept it,
And he went out to Tierci, a jongleur
And on the road for his living,
And twice he went down to Tierci,
And took off the girl there that was just married to Bernart.

And went to Auvergne, to the Dauphin,
And Tierci came with a posse to Auvergnat,
And went back for an army
And came to Auvergne with the army
But never got Pierre nor the woman.
And he went down past Chaise Dieu,
And went after it all to Mount Segur,
   after the end of all things,
And they hadn't left even the stair,
And Simone was dead by that time,
And they called us the Manicheans
Wotever the hellsarse that is.

And that was when Troy was down, all right,
        superbo Ilion...
And they were sailing along
Sitting in the stern-sheets,
Under the lee of an island
And the wind drifting off from the island.
"Tet, tet...
      what is it?" said Anchises.
"Tethnéké," said the helmsman, "I think they
"Are howling because Adonis died virgin."
"Huh! tet..." said Anchises,
      "well, they've made a bloody mess of that city."

"King Otreus, of Phrygia,
"That king is my father."
        and saw then, as of waves taking form,
As the sea, hard, a glitter of crystal,
And the waves rising but formed, holding their form.
No light reaching through them.

XXIV

THUS the book of the mandates:

Feb. 1422.

We desire that you our factors give to Zohanne of Rimini
our servant, six lire marchesini,
for the three prizes he has won racing our barbarisci,
at the rate we have agreed on. The races he has won
are the Modena, the San Petronio at Bologna
and the last race at San Zorzo.
(Signed)   Parisina Marchesa

.. pay them for binding
un libro franxese che si chiama Tristano...

Carissimi nostri
Zohanne da Rimini
has won the palio at Milan with our horse and writes that
he is now on the hotel, and wants money.
Send what you think he needs,
but when you get him back in Ferrara find out
what he has done with the first lot, I think over 25 ducats
But send the other cash quickly, as I don't want him
there on the hotel.
... perfumes, parrot seed, combs, two great and two
small ones from Venice, for madama la marxesana...
... 20 ducats to
give to a friend of ours who paid a bill for us
on this trip to Romagna...
... verde colore predeletto, 25 ducats ziparello
silver embroidered for Ugo fiolo del Signore...

(27 nov. 1427)
PROCURATIO NOMINE PATRIS, Leonello Este
(arranging dot for Margarita his sister, to
Roberto Malatesta of Rimini)
natae praelibati margaritae
Ill. D. Nicolai Marchionis Esten. et Sponsae:

The tower of Gualdo
with plenary jurisdiction in civils; and in criminal:
to fine and have scourged all delinquents
as in the rest of their lands,
"which things
this tower, estate at Gualdo had the Illustrious
Nicolaus Marquis of Este received from the said
Don Carlo (Malatesta)
for dower
Illustrae Dominae Parisinae Marxesana."

> under my hand D. Michaeli de Magnabucis
> Not. pub. Ferr.
> D. Nicolaeque Guiduccioli de Arimino.
> Sequit bonorum descriptio.

And he in his young youth, in the wake of Odysseus
To Cithera (a. d. 1413) "dove fu Elena rapta da Paris"
Dinners in orange groves, prows attended of dolphins,
Vestige of Rome at Pola, fair wind as far as Naxos
Ora vela, ora a remi, sino ad ora di vespero
Or with the sail tight hauled, by the crook'd land's arm
Zefalonia
And at Corfu, greek singers; by Rhodos
Of the windmills, and to Paphos,
Donkey boys, dust, deserts, Jerusalem, backsheesh
And an endless fuss over passports;
One groat for the Jordan, whether you go there or not,
The school where the madonna in girlhood
Went to learn letters, and Pilate's house closed to the public;
2 soldi for Olivet (to the Saracens)
And no indulgence at Judas's tree; and
"Here Christ put his thumb on a rock
"Saying: hic est medium mundi."
  (That, I assure you, happened.
          Ego, scriptor cantilenae.)
For worse? for better? but happened.
After which, the greek girls at Corfu, and the

Ladies, Venetian, and they all sang in the evening
Benche niuno cantasse, although none of them could,
Witness Luchino del Campo.
Plus one turkish juggler, and they had a bath
When they got out of Jerusalem
And for cargo: one leopard of Cyprus
And falcons, and small birds of Cyprus,
Sparrow hawks, and grayhounds from Turkey
To breed in Ferrara among thin-legged Ferrarese,
Owls, hawks, fishing tackle.

Was beheaded Aldovrandino (1425, vent'uno Maggio)
Who was cause of this evil, and after
The Marchese asked was Ugo beheaded.   And the Captain:
"Signor... si."   and il Marchese began crying
"Fa me hora tagliar la testa
"dapoi cosi presto hai decapitato il mio Ugo."
Rodendo con denti una bachetta che havea in mani.
And passed that night weeping, and calling Ugo, his son.
Affable, bullnecked, that brought seduction in place of
Rape into government, ter pacis Italiae auctor;
With the boys pulling the tow-ropes on the river
Tre cento bastardi (or bombardi fired off at his funeral)
And the next year a standard from Venice
(Where they'd called off a horse race)
And the baton from the Florentine baily.
"Of Fair aspect, gentle in manner"
Forty years old at the time;
"And they killed a judge's wife among other,
That was a judge of the court and noble,
And called Madonna Laodamia delli Romei,
Beheaded in the pa della justicia;
And in Modena, a madonna Agnesina
Who had poisoned her husband,
"All women known as adulterous,
"That his should not suffer alone."
                Then the writ ran no further.
And in '31 married Monna Ricarda.

CHARLES... scavoir faisans... et advenir... a haute
noblesse du Linage et Hostel... e faictz hautex...
vaillance... affection... notre dict Cousin...
puissance, auctorite Royal... il et ses hors yssus... et
a leur loise avoir doresenavant
A TOUSIUOURS EN LEURS ARMES ESCARTELURE
... trois fleurs Liz d'or... en champs a'asur dentelle...
ioissent et usent.
              Mil CCCC trente et ung, conseil
à Chinon, le Roy, l'Esne de la Trimouill,
Vendoise, Jehan Rabateau.

And in '32 came the Marchese Saluzzo
To visit them, his son in law and his daughter,
And to see Hercules his grandson, piccolo e putino.
And in '41 Polenta went up to Venice
Against Niccolo's caution
And was swallowed up in that city.
E fu sepulto nudo, Niccolo,
Without decoration, as ordered in testament,
Ter pacis Italiae.
And if you want to know what became of his statue,
I had a rifle class in Bondeno
And the priest sent a boy to the hardware
And he brought back the nails in a wrapping,
And it was the leaf of a diary
And he got the rest from the hardware
              (Cassini, libraio, speaking)
And on the first leaf of the wrapping
Was how in Napoleon's time
Came down a load of brass fittings from Modena
Via del Po, all went by the river,
To Piacenza for cannon, bells, door-knobs
And the statues of the Marchese Niccolo and of Borso
That were in the Piazza on columns.
And the Commendatore has made it a monograph
Without saying I told him and sent him
The name of the priest.

After him and his day
Were the cake-eaters, the consumers of icing,
That read all day per diletto
And left the night work to the servants;
Ferrara, paradiso dei sarti, "feste stomagose."

"Is it likely Divine Apollo,
That I should have stolen your cattle?
A child of my age, a mere infant,
            And besides, I have been here all night in my crib."
"Albert made me, Tura painted my wall,
And Julia the Countess sold to a tannery...

XXV

THE BOOK OF THE COUNCIL MAJOR
1255 be it enacted:
That they mustn't shoot crap in the hall
of the council, nor in the small court under
pain of 20 danari, be it enacted:
1266 no squire of Venice to throw dice
*any*where in the palace or
in the loggia of the Rialto under pain of ten soldi
or half that for kids, and if they wont pay
they are to be chucked in the water. be it enacted
In libro pactorum
To the things everlasting
memory both for live men and for the future et
quod publice innotescat
in the said date, dicto millessimo
of the illustrious lord, Lord John Soranzo
by god's grace doge of Venice in the Curia
of the Palace of the Doges,
neath the portico next the house of the dwelling of
the Castaldio and of the heralds of the Lord Doge.
being beneath same a penthouse or cages
or room timbered (trabesilis) like a cellar
one Lion male and one female *simul commorantes*
which beasts to the Lord Doge were transmitted small
by that serene Lord King Frederic of Sicily, the
said lion knew carnally and in nature the Lioness
aforesaid and impregnated in that manner that animals
leap on one another to know and impregnate
on the faith of several ocular witnesses
Which lioness bore pregnant for about three months
(as is said by those who saw her assaulted)
and in the said millessimo and month on a sunday
12th. of the month of September about sunrise on
St. Mark's day early but with the light already apparent
the said lioness as is the nature of animals
whelped per naturam three lion cubs vivos et pilosos

living and hairy which born at once began life and motion
and to go gyring about their mother throughout the
aforesaid room as saw the aforesaid Lord Doge and as it
were all the Venetians and other folk who were in
Venice that day that concurred all for this as it were
miraculous sight.   And one of the animals is a male
and the other two female

> I John Marchesini Ducal notary of the
> Venetians as eyewitness saw the
> nativity of these animals thus by
> mandate of the said Doge wrote this
> and put it in file.

Also a note from Pontius Pilate dated the "year 33."

Two columns (a. d. 1323) for the church of St. Nicholas of the
palace 12 lire gross.
To the procurators of St. Marc for entrance to the
palace, for gilding the images and the lion over the door
... to be paid...

Be it enacted:
to Donna Sorantia Soranzo that she come for the
feast of Ascension by night in a covered boat and
alight at the ripa del Palazzo, and when first sees the
Christblood go at once up into the Palace and may
stay in the Palace VIII days to visit the Doge her
father not in that time leaving the palace, nor
descending the palace stair and when she descends it
that she return by night the boat in the like manner
being covered.   To be revoked at the council's pleasure.

> accepted by 5 of the council

1335. 3 lire 15 groats to stone for making a lion.
1340. Council of the lords noble, Marc Erizio
Nic. Speranzo, Tomasso Gradonico:

> that the hall
be new built over the room of the night watch

and over the columns toward the canal where the walk is...

... because of the stink of the dungeons. 1344.
1409... since the most serene Doge can scarce
stand upright in his bedroom...
                    vadit pars, two gross lire
stone stair, 1415, for pulchritude of the palace

                              254 da parte
                                de non 23
                                4 non sincere
Which is to say: they built out over the arches
and the palace hangs there in the dawn, the mist,
in that dimness,
or as one rows in from past the murazzi
the barge slow after moon-rise
and the voice sounding under the sail.
Mist gone.
            And Sulpicia
green shoot now, and the wood
white under new cortex
"as the sculptor sees the form in the air
            before he sets hand to mallet,
"and as he sees the in, and the through,
                              the four sides
"not the one face to the painter
As ivory uncorrupted:
                    "Pone metum Cerinthe"
Lay there, the long soft grass,
            and the flute lay there by her thigh,
Sulpicia, the fauns, twig-strong,
                    gathered about her;
The fluid, over the grass
Zephyrus, passing through her,
                    "deus nec laedit amantes."
Hic mihi dies sanctus;
And from the stone pits, the heavy voices,

Heavy sound:
                    "Sero, sero...
"Nothing we made, we set nothing in order,
"Neither house nor the carving,
"And what we thought had been thought for too long;
"Our opinion not opinion in evil
"But opinion borne for too long.
"We have gathered a sieve full of water."
And from the comb of reeds, came notes and the chorus
Moving, the young fauns: Pone metum,
Metum, nec deus laedit.

And as after the form, the shadow,
Noble forms, lacking life, that bolge, that valley
the dead words keeping form,
and the cry: Civis Romanus.
The clear air, dark, dark,
The dead concepts, never the solid, the blood rite,
The vanity of Ferrara;

Clearer than shades, in the hill road
Springing in cleft of the rock: Phaethusa
There as she came among them,
Wine in the smoke-faint throat,
Fire gleam under smoke of the mountain,
Even there by meadows of Phlegethon
And against this the flute: pone metum.
Fading, that they carried their guts before them,
And thought then, the deathless,
Form, forms and renewal, gods held in the air,
Forms seen, and then clearness,
Bright void, without image, Napishtim,
Casting his gods back into the νόος.

"as the sculptor sees the form in the air...
"as glass seen under water,
"King Otreus, my father...

and saw the waves taking form as crystal,
notes as facets of air,
and the mind there, before them, moving,
so that notes needed not move.

... side toward the piazza, the worst side of the room
that no one has been willing to tackle,
and do it as cheap or much cheaper...
                    (signed)   Tician, 31 May 1513

It being convenient that there be an end to
the painting of Titian, fourth frame from the door on
the right of the hall of the greater council, begun
by maestro Tyciano da Cadore since its being thus
unfinished holds up the decoration of said hall on
the side that everyone sees.   We
move that by authority of this Council maestro Tyciano
aforesaid be constrained to finish said canvas,
and if he have not, to lose the expectancy of the
brokerage on the Fondamenta delli Thodeschi
and moreover to restore all payments recd. on account of
said canvas.   11 Aug. 1522
Ser Leonardus Emo, Sapiens Consilij:
Ser Philippus Capello, Sapiens Terrae Firmae:
In 1513 on the last day of May was conceded to
Tician of Cadore painter a succession to a brokerage
on the Fondamenta dei Thodeschi, the first to be vacant
In 1516 on the 5th. of december was declared that
without further waiting a vacancy he shd. enter that
which had been held by the painter Zuan Bellin on
condition that he paint the picture of the land battle
in the Hall of our Greater Council on the side toward
the piazza over the Canal Grande, the which Tician after
the demise of Zuan Bellin entered into possession of the
said Sensaria and has for about twenty years profited by
it, namely to about 100 ducats a year not including the
18 to 20 ducats taxes yearly remitted him it being
fitting that as he has not worked he should not have

the said profits WHEREFORE
                              be it moved that the said
Tician de Cadore, pictor, be by authority of this Council
obliged and constrained to restore to our government all the
moneys that he has had from the agency during the time he
has not worked on the painting in the said
hall as is reasonable
                ayes 102, noes 38,   37 undecided
                                        register of the senate
                                        terra 1537, carta 136.

XXVI

AND
I came here in my young youth
   and lay there under the crocodile
By the column, looking East on the Friday,
And I said: Tomorrow I will lie on the South side
And the day after, south west.
And at night they sang in the gondolas
And in the barche with lanthorns;
The prows rose silver on silver
   taking light in the darkness. "Relaxetur!"
11th. December 1461: that Pasti be let out
       with a caveat
"caveat ire ad Turchum, that he stay out of
        Constantinople
"if he hold dear our government's pleasure.
"The book will be retained by the council
   (the book being Valturio's "Re Militari").

To Nicolo Segundino, the next year, 12th. October
"Leave no... omnem... as they say... volve lapidem...
"Stone unturned that he, Pio,
"Give peace to the Malatesta.
"Faithful sons (we are) of the church
   (for two pages) ...
"And see all the cardinals and the nephew...
"And in any case get the job done.

"Our galleys were strictly neutral
"And sent there for neutrality.
"See Borso in Ferrara."
To Bernard Justinian, 28th. of October:
"Segundino is to come back with the news
"Two or three days after you get this."

Senato Secreto, 28th of October,
Came Messire Hanibal from Cesena:

"Cd. they hoist the flag of St. Mark
"And have Fortinbras and our army?"
"They cd. not... but on the quiet, secretissime,
"Two grand... Sic : He may have
"Two thousand ducats; himself to hire the men
"From our army."
. . . .
... 8 barrels wine, to Henry of Inghilterra...
Tin, serges, amber to go by us to the Levant,
Corfu, and above Corfu...

. . . .
And hither came Selvo, doge,
            that first mosiac'd San Marco,
And his wife that would touch food but with forks,
Sed aureis furculis, that is
            with small golden prongs
Bringing in, thus, the vice of luxuria;
And to greet the doge Lorenzo Tiepolo,
Barbers, heads covered with beads,
Furriers, masters in rough,
Master pelters for fine work,
And the masters for lambskin
With silver cups and their wine flasks
And blacksmiths with the gonfaron
            et leurs fioles chargies de vin,
The masters of wool cloth
Glass makers in scarlet
Carrying fabrefactions of glass;
25th April the jousting,
The Lord Nicolo Este,
            Ugaccion dei Contrarini,
The Lord Francesco Gonzaga, and first
The goldsmiths and jewelers' company
Wearing *pellande* of scarlet,
            the horses in cendato—
And it cost three ducats to rent any horse

For three hundred and fifty horses, in piazza,
And the prize was a collar with jewels
And these folk came on horses to the piazza
In the last fight fourteen on a side,
And the prize went to a nigger from Mantua
That came with Messire Gonzaga.

And that year ('38) they came here
Jan. 2.   The Marquis of Ferrara
        mainly to see the greek Emperor,
To take him down the canal to his house,
And with the Emperor came the archbishops:
The Archbishop of Morea Lower
And the Archbishop of Sardis
And the Bishops of Lacedæmon and of Mitylene,
Of Rhodos, of Modon Brandos,
And the Archbishops of Athens, Corinth, and of Trebizond,
The chief secretary and the stonolifex.
And came Cosimo Medici "almost as a Venetian to Venice"
(That would be four days later)
And on the 25th, Lord Sigismundo da Rimini
For government business
And then returned to the camp.
And in February they all packed off
To Ferrara to decide on the holy ghost
And as to the which begat the what in the Trinity. —
Gemisto and the Stonolifex,
And you would have bust your bum laughing
To see the hats and beards of those greeks.

And the guild spirit was declining.
Te fili Dux, tuosque successores
Aureo anulo, to wed the sea as a wife;
for beating the Emperor Manuel,
eleven hundred and seventy six.
1175 a. d. first bridge in Rialto.
"You may seal your acts with lead, Signor Ziani."

The jewelers company had their furs lined with scarlet
And silk cloth for the horses,
A silk cloth called cendato
That they still use for the shawls;
And at the time of that war against Hungary
Uncle Carlo Malatesta, three wounds.
Balista, sword and a lance wound;
And to our general Pandolfo, three legates,
With silk and with silver,
And with velvet, wine and confections, to keep him—
Per animarla—in mood to go on with the fighting.

"That are in San Samuele (young ladies)
          are all to go to Rialto
And to wear yellow kerchief, as are also
Their matrons (ruffiane)."
"Ambassador, for his great wisdom and money,
"That had been here as an exile, Cosimo
"Pater."
"Lord Luigi Gonzaga, to be given Casa Giustinian."

"Bishops of Lampascus and Cyprus
"And other fifty lords bishops
                              that are the church of the orient."
March 8, "That Sigismundo left Mantua
Ill contented...

And they are dead and have left a few pictures.
"Albizi have sacked the Medici bank."
"Venetians may stand, come, depart with their families
Free by land, free by sea
          in their galleys,
Ships, boats, and with merchandise.
2% on what's actually sold.   No tax above that.
          Year 6962 of the world
          18th. April, in Constantinople."
Wind on the lagoon, the south wind breaking roses.

Illmo ac ex^{mo} (eccellentissimo) princeps et d^{no}
Lord, my lord in particular, Sforza:
In reply to 1st l^{tr} of yr. ld^{shp}
re mat^r of horses, there are some for sale here.
I said that I hdn't. then seen 'em all thoroughly.
Now I may say that I have, and think
There are eleven good horses and almost that number
Of hacks that might be used in necessity,
To be had at a reasonable price.
It is true that there are X or XI big horses
    from 80 to 110 ducats
That seem to me dearer at the price
Than those for 80 ducats and under
And I think that if yr. ld^{sp} wd. send from
1000 ducats to one thousand 500 it cd. be spent
On stuff that wd. suit yr. L^{dp} quite well.
Please Y. L. to answer quickly
As I want to take myself out of here,
And if you want me to buy them
Send the cash by Mr. Pitro the farrier
And have him tell me by mouth or letter
What yr. ld^p wants me to buy.
Even from 80 ducats up there are certain good horses.
I have nothing else to say to your Lordship
Save my salutations.
Given Bologna, 14th. of August 1453
    Servant of yr. Illustrious Lordship
                             PISANELLUS

1462, 12th December: "and Vittor Capello
Brought also the head of St. George the Martyr
From the Island of Siesina.
This head was covered with silver and
Taken to San Giorgio Maggiore.

To the Cardinal Gonzaga of Mantua, ultimo febbraio 1548
"26th of feb. was killed in this city
Lorenzo de Medicis.   Yr. Illu^s L^{dshp} will understand

from the enc. account how the affair is said to have
gone off. They say those who killed him have certainly
got away in a post boat with 6 oars. But they don't
know which way they have gone, and as a guard may
have been set in certain places and passes, it wd.
be convenient if yr. Ill^s L^{dshp} wd. write at once
to your ambassador here, saying among other things
that the two men who killed Lorenzino have passed through
the city of Mantua and that no one knows which
way they have gone. Publishing this information
from yr. Ldshp will perhaps help them to get free.
Although we think they are already in Florence, but
in any case this measure can do no harm. So that
yr. Ldshp wd. benefit by doing it quickly and even
to have others send the same news.
May Our Lord protect yr. Ill^s and most Revnd person
with the increase of state you desire.

Venice, last of Feb. 1548
I kiss the hands of yr. Ill. Ld^{shp}
Don In. Hnr. de Mendoça

To the Marquis of Mantova, Fran^o Gonzaga
Illustrious my Lord, during the past few days
An unknown man was brought to me by some others
To see a Jerusalem I have made, and as soon as he
saw it he insisted that I sell it him, saying it
gave him the gtst. content and satisfac^{tn}
Finally the deal was made and he took it away,
without paying and hasn't since then appeared.
I went to tell the people who had brought him, one
of whom is a priest with a beard that wears a
grey berettino whom I have often seen with you in
the hall of the gtr. council and I asked him the
fellow's name, and it is a Messire Lorenzo, the
painter to your Lordship, from which I have easily
understood what he was up to, and on that account
I am writing you, to furnish you my name and the
work's. In the first place illustrious m. lord, I am

that painter to the Seignory, commissioned to paint the
gt. hall where Yr. Lordship deigns to mount
on the scaffold to see our work, the history of Ancona,
and my name is Victor Carpatio.
As to the Jerusalem I dare say there is not another
in our time as good and completely perfect, or as
large.   It is 25 ft. long by 5 1/2, and I know Zuane
Zamberti has often spoken of it to yr. Sublimity; I
know certainly that this painter of yours has carried
off a piece, not the whole of it.   I can send you
a small sketch in aquarelle on a roll, or have it
seen by good judges and leave the price to your
Lordship.
XV.   Aug 1511, Venetijs.

I have sent a copy of
this letter by another way to be sure you get one or the other.
The humble svt. of yr. Sublimity

Victor Carpathio
pictore.

To the supreme pig, the archbishop of Salzburg:
Lasting filth and perdition.
Since your exalted pustulence is too stingy
To give me a decent income
And has already assured me that here I have nothing to hope
And had better seek fortune elsewhere;
And since thereafter you have
Three times impeded my father and self intending departure
I ask you for the fourth time
To behave with more decency, and this time
Permit my departure.

Wolfgang Amadeus, august 1777
(inter lineas)

"As is the sonata, so is little Miss Cannabich."

XXVII

FORMANDO di disio nuova persona
One man is dead, and another has rotted his end off
Et quant au troisième
Il est tombé dans le
De sa femme, on ne le reverra
Pas, oth fugol ouitbaer:
"Observed that the paint was
Three quarters of an inch thick and concluded,
As they were being rammed through, the age of that
Cruiser."   "Referred to no longer as
The goddamned Porta-goose, but as
England's oldest ally."   "At rests in calm zone
If possible, the men are to be fed and relaxed,
The officers on the contrary..."
Ten million germs in his face,
"That is part of the risk and happens
"About twice a year in tubercular research, Dr. Spahlinger..."
"J'ai obtenu" said M. Curie, or some other scientist
"A burn that cost me six months in curing,"
And continued his experiments.
England off there in black darkness,
Russia off there in black darkness,
The last crumbs of civilization...
And they elected a Prince des Penseurs
Because there were so damn many princes,
And they elected a Monsieur Brisset
Who held that man is descended from frogs;
And there was a cracked concierge that they
Nearly got into the Deputies,
To protest against the earthquake in Messina.
   The Bucentoro sang it in that year,
1908, 1909, 1910, and there was
An old washerwoman beating her washboard,
That would be 1920, with a cracked voice,
Singing "Stretti!" and that was the last
Till this year, '27, Hotel Angioli, in Milan,
With an air Clara d'Ellébeuse,

With their lakelike and foxlike eyes,
With an air "Benette joue la Valse des Elfes"
In the salotto of that drummer's hotel,
Two young ladies with their air de province:
"No, we are Croat merchants, commercianti,
"There is nothing strange in our history."
"No, not to sell, but to buy."

And there was that music publisher,
The fellow that brought back the shrunk Indian head
Boned, oiled, from Bolivia, said:
"Yes, I went out there. Couldn't make out the trade,
Long after we'd melt up the plates,
Get an order, 200 copies, Peru,
Or some station in Chile."
Took out Floradora in sheets,
And brought back a red-headed mummy.
With an air Clara d'Ellébeuse, singing "Stretti."

Sed et universus quoque ecclesie populus,
All rushed out and built the duomo,
Went as one man without leaders
And the perfect measure took form;
"Glielmo ciptadin" says the stone, "the author,
"And Nicolao was the carver"
Whatever the meaning may be.
And they wrote for year after year.
Refining the criterion,
Or they rose as the tops subsided;
Brumaire, Fructidor, Petrograd.
And Tovarisch lay in the wind
And the sun lay over the wind,
And three forms became in the air
And hovered about him,
                    so that he said:
This machinery is very ancient,
                    surely we have heard this before.
And the waves like a forest

Where the wind is weightless in the leaves
But moving,
   so that the sound runs upon sound.
   Xarites, born of Venus and wine.

Carved stone upon stone.
But in sleep, in the waking dream,
Petal'd the air;
   twig where but wind-streak had been;
Moving bough without root,
       by Helios.
So that the Xarites bent over tovarisch.
And these are the labours of tovarisch,
That tovarisch lay in the earth,
And rose, and wrecked the house of the tyrants,
And that tovarisch then lay in the earth
   And the Xarites bent over tovarisch.

These are the labours of tovarisch,
That tovarisch wrecked the house of the tyrants,
And rose, and talked folly on folly,
And walked forth and lay in the earth
   And the Xarites bent over tovarisch.

And that tovarisch cursed and blessed without aim,
   These are the labours of tovarisch,
Saying:
   "Me Cadmus sowed in the earth
   And with the thirtieth autumn
I return to the earth that made me.
Let the five last build the wall;

I neither build nor reap.
That he came with the gold ships, Cadmus,
That he fought with the wisdom,
Cadmus, of the gilded prows.   Nothing I build
And I reap
Nothing; with the thirtieth autumn

I sleep, I sleep not, I rot
And I build no wall.
            Where was the wall of Eblis
At Ventadour, there now are the bees,
And in that court, wild grass for their pleasure
That they carry back to the crevice
Where loose stone hangs upon stone.
I sailed never with Cadmus,
            lifted never stone above stone."

"Baked and eaten tovarisch!
"Baked and eaten, tovarisch, my boy,
"That is your story.   And up again,
"Up and at 'em.   Laid never stone upon stone."

"The air burst into leaf."
"Hung there flowered acanthus,
"Can you tell the down from the up?"

XXVIII

AND God the Father Eternal (Boja d'un Dio!)
Having made all things he cd.
think of, felt yet
That something was lacking, and thought
Still more, and reflected that
The Romagnolo was lacking, and
Stamped with his foot in the mud and
Up comes the Romagnolo:
        "Gard, yeh bloudy 'angman! It's me."
Aso iqua me. All Esimo Dottor Aldo Walluschnig
Who with the force of his intellect
With art and assiduous care
Has snatched from death by a most perilous operation
The classical Caesarean cut
Marotti, Virginia, in Senni of San Giorgio
At the same time saving her son.
May there move to his laud the applause of all men
And the gratitude of the family.
        S. Giorgio, 23d May. A.D. 1925.
Item: There are people that can swimme in the sea
Havens and rivers naked
Having bowes and shafts,
Coveting to draw nigh yr. shippe which if they find not
Well watched and warded they wil assault
Desirous of the bodies of men which they covet for meate,
If you resist them
    They dive and wil flee.
And Mr Lourpee sat on the floor of the pension dining-room
Or perhaps it was in the alcove
And about him lay a great mass of pastells,
That is, stubbs and broken pencils of pastell,
In pale indeterminate colours.
And he admired the Sage of Concord
    "Too broad ever to make up his mind."
And the mind of Lourpee at fifty
Directed him into a room with a certain vagueness

As if he wd.
neither come in nor stay out
As if he wd.
go neither to the left nor the right
And his painting reflected this habit.
And Mrs Kreffle's mind was made up,
Perhaps by the pressure of circumstance,
She described her splendid apartment
In Paris and left without paying her bill
And in fact she wrote later from Sevilla
And requested a shawl, and received it
From the Senora at 300 pesetas cost to the latter
(Also without remitting) which
May have explained the lassitude of her daughter;
And the best paid dramatic critic
Arrived from Manhattan
And was lodged in a bordello (promptly)
Having trusted "his people"
Who trusted a Dutch correspondent,
And when they had been devoured by fleas
(Critic and family)
They endeavoured to break the dutchman's month's contract,
And the ladies from West Virginia
Preserved the natal aroma,
And in the railway feeding-room in Chiasso
She sat as if waiting for the train for Topeka
—That was the year of the strikes—
When we came up toward Chiasso
By the last on the narrow-gauge,
Then by tramway from Como
Leaving the lady who loved bullfights
With her eight trunks and her captured hidalgo,
And a dutchman was there who was going
To take the boat at Trieste,
Sure, he was going to take it;
Would he go round by Vienna? He would not.
Absence of trains wdnt. stop him.

So we left him at last in Chiasso
Along with the old woman from Kansas,
Solid Kansas, her daughter had married that Swiss
Who kept the buffet in Chiasso.
Did it shake her?   It did not shake her.
She sat there in the waiting room, solid Kansas,
Stiff as a cigar-store indian from the Bowery
Such as one saw in "the nineties,"
First sod of bleeding Kansas
That had produced this ligneous solidness;
If thou wilt go to Chiasso wilt find that indestructable female
As if waiting for the train to Topeka
In the buffet of that station on the bench that
Follows the wall, to the right side as you enter.
And Clara Leonora wd. come puffing so that one
Cd. hear her when she reached the foot of the stairs,
Squared, chunky, with her crooked steel spectacles
And her splutter and her face full of teeth
And old Rennert wd. sigh heavily
And look over the top of his lenses and
She wd. arrive after due interval with a pinwheel
Concerning Grillparzer or—pratzer
Or whatever follow the Grill —, and il Gran Maestro
Mr Liszt had come to the home of her parents
And taken her on his prevalent knee and
She held that a sonnet was a sonnet
And ought never be destroyed,
And had taken a number of courses
And continued with hope of degrees and
Ended in a Baptist learnery
          Somewhere near the Rio Grande.

And they wanted more from their women,
Wanted 'em jacked up a little
And sent over for teachers (Ceylon)
So Loica went out and died there
After her time in the post-Ibsen movement.

And one day in Smith's room
Or may be it was that 1908 medico's
Put the gob in the fire-place
Ole Byers and Feigenbaum and Joe Bromley,
Joe hittin' the gob at 25 feet
Every time, ping on the metal
        (Az ole man Comley wd. say: Boys!...
        Never cherr terbakker! Hrwwkke tth!
        Never cherr terbakker!,
"Missionaries," said Joe, "I was out back of Jaffa,
I dressed in the costume, used to like the cafés,
All of us settin' there on the ground,
Pokes his head in the doorway: "Iz there any,"
He says, "Gar'
Damn
Man here
Thet kan speak ENGLISH?"
        Nobody said anything fer a while
And then I said: "Hu er' you?"
"I'm er misshernary I am"
He sez, "chucked off a naval boat in Shanghaï.
I worked at it three months, nothin' to live on."
Beat his way overland.
I never saw the twenty I lent him."

Great moral secret service, plan, Tribune is told
limit number to thirty thousand,
only highest type will be included,
propaganda within ranks of the veterans,
to keep within bounds when they come into
contact with personal liberty...with the french authorities...
that includes the Paris police...
Strengthen franco-american amity.

NARCOTIC CHARGE: Frank Robert Iriquois
gave his home Oklahoma City... Expelled July 24 th.

"Je suis...
(Across the bare planks of a diningroom in the Pyrenees)
        ... plus fort que...
                        ... le Boud-hah!"
(No contradiction)
"Je suis...
        ... plus fort que le...
                        ... Christ!
(No contradiction)
"J'aurais...
        aboli...
                le poids!"
(Silence, somewhat unconvinced.)
And in his waste house, detritus,
As it were the cast buttons of splendours,
The harbour of Martinique, drawn every house, and in detail.
Green shutters on half the houses,
Half the thing still unpainted.
                        "... sont
"l'in.. fan... terie KOH-
                lon-
                        i-ale"

voce tinnula
"Ce sont les vieux Marsouins!"
He made it, feitz Marcebrus, the words and the music,
Uniform out for Peace Day
And that lie about the Tibetan temple
(happens by the way to be true,
they do carry you up on their shoulders) but
Bad for his medical practice.
"Retreat?" said Dr Wymans, "It was marrvelous...
Gallipoli...
Secret. Turks knew nothing about it.
Uh! Helped me to get my wounded aboard."
And that man sweat blood to put through that railway,
And what he ever got out of it?

And one day he drove down to the whorehouse
Cause all the farmers had consented
                    and granted the right of way,
But the pornoboskos wdn't. have it at any price
And said he'd shoot the surveyors,
But he didn't shoot ole pop in the buckboard,
He giv him the right of way.
And they thought they had him flummox'd,
Nobody'd sell any rails;
Till he went up to the north of New York state
And found some there on the ground
And he had 'em pried loose and shipped 'em
And had 'em laid here through the forest.

Thing is to find something simple
As for example Pa Stadtvolk;
Hooks to hang gutters on roofs,
A spike and half-circle, patented 'em and then made 'em;
Worth a good million, not a book in the place;
Got a horse about twenty years after, seen him
                    Of a Saturday afternoon
When they'd taken down an old fence,
Ole Pa out there knockin the nails out
(To *save* 'em). I hear he smoked good cigars.

And when the Prince Oltrepassimo died, saccone,
That follow the coffins,
He lay there on the floor of the chapel
On a great piece of patterned brocade
And the walls solid gold about him
And there was a hole in one of his socks
And the place open that day to the public,
Kids running in from the street
And a cat sat there licking himself
And then stepped over the Principe,
Discobolus upstairs and the main door
Not opened since '70
When the Pope shut himself into the Vatican

And they had scales on the table
To weigh out the food on fast days;
And he lay there with his hood back
And the hole in one of his socks.

"Buk!" said the Second Baronet, "eh...
"Thass a funny lookin' buk" said the Baronet
Looking at Bayle, folio, 4 vols. in gilt leather, "Ah...
"Wu... Wu... wot you goin' eh to do with ah...
"... ah read-it?"
                    Sic loquitur eques.

And lest it pass with the day's news
Thrown out with the daily paper,
Neither official pet
Nor Levine with the lucky button
Went on into darkness,
Saw naught above but close dark,
Weight of ice on the fuselage
Borne into the tempest, black cloud wrapping their wings,
The night hollow beneath them
And fell with dawn into ocean
But for the night saw neither sky nor ocean
And found ship... why?... how?... by the Azores.
And she was a bathing beauty, Miss Arkansas or Texas
And the man (of course) quasi anonymous
Neither a placard for non-smokers or non-alcohol
Nor for the code of Peoria;
Or one-eyed Hinchcliffe and Elsie
Blackeyed bitch that married dear Dennis,
That flew out into nothingness
And her father was the son of one too
That got the annulment.

XXIX

PEARL, great sphere, and hollow,
Mist over lake, full of sunlight,
Pernella concubina
The sleeve green and shot gold over her hand
Wishing her son to inherit
Expecting the heir ainé be killed in battle
He being courageous, poisoned his brother puiné
Laying blame on Siena
And this she did by a page
Bringing war once more on Pitigliano
And the page repented and told this
To Nicolo (ainé) Pitigliano
Who won back that rock from his father
"still doting on Pernella his concubine."
       The sand that night like a seal's back
       Glossy beneath the lanthorns.
From the Via Sacra
       (fleeing what band of Tritons)
Up to the open air
Over that mound of the hippodrome:
Liberans et vinculo ab omni liberatos
As who with four hands at the cross roads
By king's hand or sacerdos'
       are given their freedom
—Save who were at Castra San Zeno...

Cunizza for God's love, for remitting the soul of her father
—May hell take the traitors of Zeno.
And fifth begat he Alberic
And sixth the Lady Cunizza.
       In the house of the Cavalcanti
              anno 1265:
Free go they all as by full manumission
All serfs of Eccelin my father da Romano
Save those who were with Alberic at Castra San Zeno
And let them go also
The devils of hell in their body.

And sixth the Lady Cunizza
That was first given Richard St Boniface
And Sordello subtracted her from that husband
And lay with her in Tarviso
Till he was driven out of Tarviso
And she left with a soldier named Bonius
nimium amorata in eum
And went from one place to another
"The light of this star o'ercame me"
Greatly enjoying herself
And running up the most awful bills.
And this Bonius was killed on a sunday
and she had then a Lord from Braganza
and later a house in Verona.

And he looked from the planks to heaven,
Said Juventus: "Immortal...
He said: "Ten thousand years before now...
Or he said: "Passing into the point of the cone
You begin by making the replica.
Thus Lusty Juventus, in September,
In cool air, under sky,
Before the residence of the funeral director
Whose daughters' conduct caused comment.
But the old man did not know how he felt
Nor cd. remember what prompted the utterance.
He said: "What I know, I have known,
"How can the knowing cease knowing?"
By the lawn of the senior elder
He continued his ambulation:
"Matter is the lightest of all things,
"Chaff, rolled into balls, tossed, whirled in the aether,
"Undoubtedly crushed by the weight,
"Light also proceeds from the eye;
"In the globe over my head
"Twenty feet in diameter, thirty feet in diameter
"Glassy, the glaring surface—
"There are many reflections

"So that one may watch them turning and moving
"With heads down now, and now up.
He went on toward the amateur student of minerals
That later went bankrupt;
He went on past the house of the local funny man,
Jo Tyson that had a camera.   His daughter was bow-legged
And married the assembly-man's son.

      O-hon dit que-ke fois au vi'-a-ge...

Past the house of the three retired clergymen
Who were too cultured to keep their jobs.
Languor has cried unto languor
      about the marshmallow-roast
(Let us speak of the osmosis of persons)
The wail of the phonograph has penetrated their marrow
(Let us...
The wail of the pornograph....)
    The cicadas continue uninterrupted.
With a vain emptiness the virgins return to their homes
With a vain exasperation
The ephèbe has gone back to his dwelling,
The djassban has hammered and hammered,
The gentleman of fifty has reflected
      That it is perhaps just as well.
Let things remain as they are.
The mythological exterior lies on the moss in the forest
And questions him about Darwin.
And with a burning fire of phantasy
      he replies with "Deh! nuvoletta..."
So that she would regret his departure.
      Drift of weed in the bay:
She seeking a guide, a mentor,
He aspires to a career with honour
To step in the tracks of his elders;
      a greater incomprehension?
There is no greater incomprehension
Than between the young and the young.

The young seek comprehension;
The middleaged to fulfill their desire.
Sea weed dried now, and now floated,
          mind drifts, weed, slow youth, drifts,
Stretched on the rock, bleached and now floated;
Wein, Weib, TAN AOIDAN
Chiefest of these the second, the female
Is an element, the female
Is a chaos
An octopus
A biological process
                    and we seek to fulfill...
TAN AOIDAN, our desire, drift...
               Ailas e que'm fau miey huelh
               Quar no vezon so qu'ieu vuelh.
Our mulberry leaf, woman, TAN AOIDAN,
"Nel ventre tuo, o nella mente mia,
"Yes, Milady, precisely, if you wd.
have anything properly made."

"Faziamo tutte le due...
"No, not in the palm-room."   The lady says it is
Too cold in the palm-room.   Des valeurs,
Nom de Dieu, et
     encore des valeurs.

She is submarine, she is an octopus, she is
A biological process,
So Arnaut turned there
Above him the wave pattern cut in the stone
Spire-top alevel the well-curb
And the tower with cut stone above that, saying:
     "I am afraid of the life after death."
and after a pause:
"Now, at last, I have shocked him."
And another day or evening toward sundown by the arena
(les gradins)
A little lace at the wrist

And not very clean lace either...
And I, "But this beats me,
"Beats me, I mean that I do not understand it;
"This love of death that is in them."
       Let us consider the osmosis of persons
nondum orto jubare;
The tower, ivory, the clear sky
Ivory rigid in sunlight
And the pale clear of the heaven
Phoibos of narrow thighs,
The cut cool of the air,
Blossom cut on the wind, by Helios
Lord of the Light's edge, and April
Blown round the feet of the God,
Beauty on an ass-cart
Sitting on five sacks of laundry
That wd. have been the road by Perugia
That leads out to San Piero. Eyes brown topaz,
Brookwater over brown sand,
The white hounds on the slope,
Glide of water, lights and the prore,
Silver beaks out of night,
Stone, bough over bough,
       lamps fluid in water,
Pine by the black trunk of its shadow
And on hill black trunks of the shadow
The trees melted in air.

XXX

COMPLEYNT, compleynt I hearde upon a day,
Artemis singing, Artemis, Artemis
Agaynst Pity lifted her wail:
Pity causeth the forests to fail,
Pity slayeth my nymphs,
Pity spareth so many an evil thing.
Pity befouleth April,
Pity is the root and the spring.
Now if no fayre creature followeth me
It is on account of Pity,
It is on account that Pity forbideth them slaye.
All things are made foul in this season,
This is the reason, none may seek purity
Having for foulnesse pity
And things growne awry;
No more do my shaftes fly
To slay.   Nothing is now clean slayne
But rotteth away.

In Paphos, on a day
                    I also heard:
... goeth not with young Mars to playe
But she hath pity on a doddering fool,
She tendeth his fyre,
She keepeth his embers warm.

Time is the evil.   Evil.
                    A day, and a day
Walked the young Pedro baffled,
                    a day and a day
After Ignez was murdered.

Came the Lords in Lisboa
                    a day, and a day
In homage.   Seated there
                    dead eyes,

: 347 :

Dead hair under the crown,
The King still young there beside her.

Came Madame "ΥΛΗ
Clothed with the light of the altar
And with the price of the candles.
"Honour?   Balls for yr. honour!
Take two million and swallow it."
                    Is come Messire Alfonso
And is departed by boat for Ferrara
And has passed here without saying "O."

Whence have we carved it in metal
Here working in Caesar's fane:
            To the Prince Caesare Borgia
            Duke of Valent and Aemelia
...and here have I brought cutters of letters
and printers not vile and vulgar
            (in Fano Caesaris)
notable and sufficient compositors
and a die-cutter for greek fonts and hebrew
named Messire Francesco da Bologna
not only of the usual types but he hath excogitated
a new form called cursive or chancellry letters
nor was it Aldous nor any other but it was
this Messire Francesco who hath cut all Aldous his letters
with such grace and charm as is known
            Hieronymous Soncinus 7th July 1503.
and as for text we have taken it
from that of Messire Laurentius
and from a codex once of the Lords Malatesta...

And in August that year died Pope Alessandro Borgia,
            Il Papa mori.

Explicit canto
XXX